AILING OFF
HE BEACH

D1440174

Other Adlard Coles titles by Alan Watts

Instant Weather Forecasting

ISBN 0 229 11724 4

A long-time classic, this revolutionary book,
which includes 24 colour photographs of cloud
formations, is a guide to forecasting weather
in the hours ahead. It enables the user to
predict, with reasonable accuracy, whether it
will rain or blow, whether conditions will
remain unchanged or perhaps clear up soon.

Instant Wind Forecasting

ISBN 0 229 11830 5

A companion to *Instant Weather Forecasting*,
this book is a ready reckoner for all who work
or play outdoors, whether dinghy, coastal or
offshore sailors. Twenty-four colour
photographs enable the reader to make
meaningful predictions as to how the wind
will behave, based on the look of the sky and
feel of the day.

*Reading the Weather: Modern Techniques for
Yachtsmen*

ISBN 0 229 11774 0

As new forecasting hardware becomes
cheaper so items such as weather fax will
become common aboard boats. This definitive
work explains the use of modern equipment as
well as the principles of reading the weather
signs for safer, more efficient and more
competitive sailing. For cruising and racing
sailors.

Alan Watts

SAILING OFF
THE BEACH

*A POCKET COMPANION
FOR DINGHY AND BOARD SAILORS*

ADLARD COLES
8 Grafton Street, London W1

Adlard Coles
William Collins Sons & Co.
8 Grafton Street, London W

First published in Great Britain by
Adlard Coles 1990

Copyright © Alan Watts 1990

British Library Cataloguing in Publication Data
Watts, Alan *1925–*
   Sailing off the beach: for dinghy and board sailors.
   1. Sailing dinghies. Sailing   2. Wind surfing
   I. Title
   797.1'24
ISBN 0–229–11865–8

Phototypeset by Computape (Pickering) Ltd, North Yorkshire
Printed and bound in Great Britain by
Hartnolls Ltd, Bodmin, Cornwall

CONTENTS

Everyone who sails a small craft does so from some beach or other. A beach, in this context, is wherever the water and the land meet. It may be straight onto the open sea or from the edges of what is sometimes a muddy creek. It can be from the drift-wood strewn edge of a large lake or reservoir, or it can be from the sides of what, by comparison, is just a pond.

Wherever your beach is it occupies that odd zone of weather which is sometimes characteristic of the water and at other times just like the land. Which way the wind blows with respect to the beach makes a world of difference to the conditions you can expect, and with a weather forecast and a map you can often avoid the situation where you set out to go sailing only to find the conditions are not the ones you like.

The advent of the sailboard and the car-top dinghy have meant that many people now sail without the advantages (or drawbacks) of belonging to a recognised sailing club. Any piece of water that is open to the public and which has launching facilities is now somewhere to sail. This way you are on your own and need to keep safety well in mind if you plan to sail alone. I have imagined this lone sail on an unfamiliar bit of water in many of the remarks and suggestions made in this book. I have also given the briefest of instruction on sailing dinghies and boards so that, should you borrow or hire a craft not having done much sailing before, you can make something of your first sorties.

If you are an improver or an expert the hints on how to look at a coastline and make up your mind where to sail – and where not to – should help to improve your score of days when you get the right conditions, whether you seek winds under Force 4 or over. When you go to a new stretch of coast, whether at home or abroad, it helps to know what chance there is of getting the winds you want. Part Two is a unique guide to all the coasts of Britain, Atlantic Europe, the Baltic and the Mediterranean. In this section you will find the frequency of winds of different strengths throughout the year, as well as likely sea temperatures, so you will know what protective clothing you may need.

It is possible that more boardsailors do their thing on inland waters than from around the coastline and so the special conditions of lakes, reservoirs, rivers and canals need to be kept in mind. Nasty things can happen on inland water that are undreamed of by the seaside beach sailor.

The inland sailor has no problem with tides and rarely with waves, but these are important phenomena for the coastal sailor, whether you are sailing straight onto the open sea or from the shores of a creek or estuary. Understanding the tidal regime is important to the peripatetic sailor who may want to visit several different venues in a season. To arrive at a coastal inlet to find nothing but mud is, to say the least, frustrating. Not being able to launch through the surf is also something to be borne in mind when setting out for a coastal sail.

These topics and many others of importance to small-craft sailors are covered in this book which I hope many will find helpful, whether they be beginner, improver or expert. I hope it brings together in one place those pieces of knowledge that make for happy and successful sailing whether you sail on your own, or with a club, at home or abroad.

Note – to avoid confusion, *offshore* means 'further out from the shore' while *off-shore*, when applied to wind direction, means 'blowing from the shore to the water'. Likewise, *on-shore* means 'blowing from water to land'.

Alan Watts
April 1990

PART ONE
1   DINGHIES AND BOARDS

Sailing an easily transportable small craft means that you will either be sailing a dinghy or a sailboard. The latter have shown a phenomenal growth over the last few years because they are cheap, efficient and fun. Their most saleable attribute is, however, the ease with which they can be carried on a car, rigged and sailed. Dinghies tend to be more complicated and many are too heavy to go on the roof of a normal car and so need to be towed on a special trailer. Even so there are a large number of car-top dinghies being sailed on all kinds of water around the world.

In a book like this there is not room to give more than the rudiments of sailing dinghies or boards – and the techniques are different. With a dinghy you have a fixed mast and when the mast careens, so does the craft. To steer it you use a rudder. On a board your mast is not fixed and can flop about anywhere while the board does its own thing. You have to steer it by using the force on the sails which you swing forwards of the centre of lateral resistance (around the position of the daggerboard cassette) to bear away from the wind, or swing aft to bring the board onto the wind. You cannot, however expert you may become, fly a dinghy into the air as you can a sailboard. The two craft are not the same, but what they have in common is that they use the wind acting on a curved aerofoil section (the sail) to create forward way.

If you have never sailed before, or are very new to sailing, and are offered the use of dinghy or a board – or you hire or buy one – do get some form of tuition first. You can make yourself look something of a fool if you set sail without a thought and then have to be rescued as you drift into the sunset.

It is more essential to get board sailing tuition than dinghy tuition. This is because in your initial trips in a dinghy it will not constantly tip you into the water as the board will. A dinghy will allow you to make some kind of stab at sailing if you take care to choose a light wind and follow some simple initial rules.

Points of sailing

Because of the way the wind acts on the sails to produce force, a dinghy or board cannot sail closer to the wind than a certain angle. This angle is assumed to be 45° either side of the wind direction (Fig. 1.1). There is therefore a 'no-go zone' and if you point the bows into it the sails will lose driving force, the foresail (if you have one) will shiver and refuse to *draw* and if you do not *bear away* you will lose way and begin to drift astern. (See Glossary on p. 8 for explanation of these terms.)

Fig. 1.1 The points of sailing

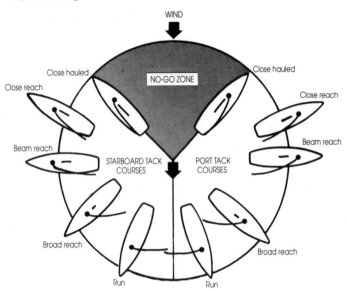

CLOSE HAULED

When you sail as close to the wind as is practicable, keeping the sails drawing nicely and varying your course slightly to allow for the little shifts there are in the wind, then you are 'sailing close-hauled' or you are 'on the wind'. The process of continually tacking so as to make way to windward is called 'beating to windward' – the term carries the second message that hard work is often involved.

If the wind blows in over the left side of the boat then you are on 'port tack', and when it comes in over the right side, 'starboard tack'. Thus as in Fig. 1.1 all courses sailed to the left of the wind are starboard tack courses while those to the right are port tack courses.

In the diagrams in this book a line where the centreboard case is situated indicates:

- board fully down – long line;
- board half-way down – short line;
- board up or almost up – no line.

So to provide maximum side area and so reduce *leeway* you need the board right down when beating. Making maximum way to windward is the most difficult of arts and is usually where sailing races are won or lost.

CLOSE REACHING

By bearing away a little from the close-hauled situation you are said to be close reaching. This is the fastest point of sailing for planing dinghies and boards. The sails are eased a little to keep the maximum flow in them and you can use a little less centreboard. Be ready for the sudden acceleration of a planing dinghy in moderate winds as you suddenly go from *displacement sailing* on the wind to planing off it.

BEAM REACHING

When you sail a course across the *true wind direction* then you are beam reaching. However, the racing flag will not tell you whether you are actually across the true wind because it streams along the *apparent wind* direction. Thus you will only know if you are truly beam reaching if you have looked at where the true wind is coming from before starting and landmarks at a considerable distance at right angles to that. Not that it matters too much. You simply bear away more from the close-hauled course, ease the sheets (or on boards let out the boom with the sail hand) and haul your centreboard half up. On boards in light winds it may be best to leave the daggerboard down so that its side area makes the board more laterally stable.

BROAD REACHING

Here you have the true wind coming over the *quarter*. The sheets must be eased considerably and you need even less centreboard. This is a slower point of sailing for dinghies. The reason lies in the *'slot' effect* of the foresail having less efficiency as the boat comes away from the wind.

RUNNING

If the wind is dead behind you then you are on a 'dead run'. This is a difficult point of sailing for dinghies and may be almost impossible for some boards. Dinghies have a choice of which tack to be on; they may have their mainsails fully out to one side or the other and it does not matter very often which. However, on gusty days it is better to have the boom out to starboard when forced onto a dead run. The foresail should be *goosewinged*, i.e. spread on the opposite side to the mainsail to present the maximum sail area to the wind. Dinghies should have their centreboards fully up unless, as with boards, it is felt that some side area under the craft will ease rolling. However, neither dinghies nor boards should have full keel when running in anything like a moderate wind or more.

Sailing to either side of the dead run course has advantages. The dinghy travels faster and there is less danger of *gybing*. So 'tacking down wind' can be a good thing to do both for beginners and experts. On short boards it is essential, and it helps on all-round or competition boards. At the end of each running leg you gybe the boom over. For example in Fig. 1.1 after a starboard tack run you gybe over and make a port tack run and so on. However, gybing can be a hazardous occupation in strong winds and a safer alternative is to *come about* on the tack you are on and then run off on the opposite tack. The gybing manoeuvre is easier for sailboarders as they just let the boom swing through over the bow of the board and sheet in on the new running course. Boards should have some, but not full, daggerboard to help control the often alarming rolling that may occur when running before the wind.

Starting to sail a dinghy

Given a fairly stiff dinghy and a light wind newcomers cannot come to much harm. It is not like a sailboard where you are in constant danger of falling off while you are learning. Even so, you will learn to sail a dinghy much more rapidly if you do just a little forward thinking about the wind. Do not fall into the trap of becoming a 'Lee shore Charlie', in that you do not point the boat in the correct direction to make it sail into the wind and also forget how important the centreboard is. If you do not take account of these two factors you will always end up being pushed further and further away from the direction of the wind. Some small waves will not be such a drawback as they are when learning to sail a board. Adopt the following technique.

1. Before you go afloat stand on the shore and face the wind direction.

2. Stretch your arms out equally in front of you so they form a right angle. You cannot sail within that right angle – it is the no-go zone.

3. Note features on the horizon that your fingers are pointing at. Then, when you get afloat, sail just a little outside those markers and you will be close to being on the wind without the risk of constantly having the wind coming ahead of you, backwinding the sails and making you lose way. The features may be landmarks on the other side of the bay or lake such as trees or a chimney, the end of the pier, buoys or anchored boats. So long as they are a good distance away you will not have to relocate them providing you do not sail far along the shore. On inland waters you will always have some landmarks you can latch onto so that you can learn to sail to windward.

Remember that when you tack (by pushing the tiller away from you – see Fig. 1.2) you want to centralise the rudder and haul in on the mainsheet and foresheet before the bow crosses the landmark you have chosen for the other tack. Tack quite often at first to get used to doing it and so you do not wander too far from where you started. Note how the tide is setting along the shore and carrying you one way or the

Fig. 1.2 The parts of a dinghy and its sails. The sides and corners of the foresail have the same names as the mainsail

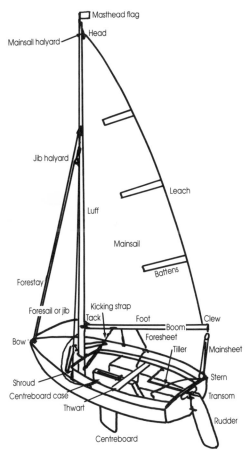

other. Sail against the tide whenever you can, and certainly on a river or a tidal creek always sail against the stream so that you can get back easily.

As the wind shifts you constantly have to push the dinghy's bows off the wind when the sails start to shiver, but you can then try bringing the bow back to its original direction so as to stay on the wind. To reach across the wind just let your sails out further, but not too far – you only have the sails fully out when running before the wind. You can tell where the wind is coming from by the masthead flag, but remember that it is the apparent wind that the flag shows, and not the true wind which was the one you used as your basic direction on the beach to find the no-go zone.

STRONGER WINDS

I am assuming that you have the sense not to try to learn to sail in a wind that is too strong for you, but as you gain confidence you will want to sample stronger winds. In light winds you can leave the centreboard down all the time, whichever point of sailing you are on, but in stronger winds you need to raise it about halfway when sailing across the wind (reaching) and can have it almost up when running. If the boat planes across the wind, then having a full centreboard down may lead to an unexpected capsize.

If you do go out in winds that make the boat plane then shift your weight further aft during the planes and move more centrally when it comes off the plane.

GYBING

It is a good idea to sail figure of eight courses when you are learning so as to become familiar not only with tacking, but also with gybing. You should learn to gybe in light winds first as a dinghy is more likely to capsize on this manoeuvre than any other.

Basically to gybe you must pull the tiller towards yourself at the same time as you let the sheets run out. They should be fully out when the boat comes tail to wind, then allow for the boom swinging sharply across the craft and for the dinghy to try to come round into the wind. This must be countered by the rudder so that the boat swings onto the new tack smoothly as you gather in the sheets.

Do not try running dead before the wind at first or you may get an unexpected gybe – and an unexpected ducking. Sail across the dead run direction, i.e. on a broad run, and gybe when you want to get back again towards the point you are aiming for.

WHEN YOU FIRST SAIL A DINGHY

Go out with someone who knows the ropes, or read up about it first.

Choose a light wind that blows on-shore – mornings are often best.

Make sure you can 'go about' before you get far from the shore.

Do not sail when big cauliflower-headed clouds build about the sky (see Photo 1).

Once you have gained confidence read about the pitfalls off beaches etc. and do not chance your luck.

If you get into difficulty lower the sail and sit it out – *never* try to swim ashore.

RIGHTING FROM A CAPSIZE

When a dinghy capsizes in winds that are not very strong it often does so slowly enough for you to climb up onto the weather gun'l (the side from which the wind is blowing) – you sometimes need not even get wet. With the centreboard down you can then climb down and stand on the centreboard so that the dinghy rights itself at the same time as you scramble in. You can support yourself in this manoeuvre by grabbing hold of the foresheet and coming in hand over hand as the craft comes upright.

All the above are the simplest details of how to sail and right a dinghy. There are many good books available that explain how to take your sailing further, but when you do go sailing always obey the rules about clothing and personal buoyancy as well as the rules of the road and the beach (see page 90).

Photo 1 When deep cauliflower-headed clouds are about allow for the strong gusts that they bring. Look for rain 'stalks' (centre right), which is often where the strongest wind is.

Glossary of sailing terms

Apparent wind direction – is the direction of the wind induced by the craft's forward way. It is always *ahead* of the true wind direction.

Beam – the beam is the direction across the craft.

Bearing away – you bear away when you turn away from the wind direction.

Coming about – you come about when you tack through the wind direction. (You can produce the same effect by gybing but coming about is reserved for turning *through* the wind.)

Displacement sailing – is when the craft rides between the two waves that are induced by its forward way. It occurs at low speeds.

Draw – the sails are said to draw when they are just full of wind and not fluttering or flapping.

Goosewinged – you are goosewinged when the foresail is set on the opposite side to the mainsail during a dead run.

Gybing – is a tacking procedure where the craft turns away from the wind rather than towards it as occurs in normal tacking.

Leeward – the side away from the wind.

Leeway – is the unwanted sideways movement that makes the craft crab slightly away from the course being steered.

Planing – a dinghy or board is planing when the after of the two waves made when displacement sailing does not touch the stern of the craft. Speed and hull shape lead to planing. Long thin hulls plane in lower wind speeds than short fat ones.

Quarter – is the part of the craft between the beam and the stern.

Slot effect – occurs when there are two sails and the foresail is used to compress and speed up the airflow over the leeward side of the mainsail.

True wind direction – is the direction of the wind when the craft is stationary.

Windward – the direction from which the wind comes.

Starting to sail a board

Even for those who can sail dinghies the technique of sailing a board is so different that they should go to a school and learn the rudiments. However, many people may not be able to attend a boardsailing school, or maybe just want to try out a hired or borrowed board. So if board sailing is new to you here are a few tips:

1. Choose the right conditions – that means a light wind and no waves. The light wind will be enough to pull against so you can support yourself on the board and the lack of waves will stop you being continually tipped off by them. You will fall off enough in flat water without the added hazard of even slight waves. Your best time is often just after breakfast when the wind is just getting up, but has not had time to

create waves. Better still find a backwater or a lagoon, canal or reservoir where you will not have waves anyway.

2. Position the board across the wind with the mast lying on the water away from you and the uphaul in both hands (see Fig. 1.3). If the board will not stay in that position try to get someone to hold it for you. Have the daggerboard down as far as possible – it will help to keep the board stable.

3. Haul the rig up hand over hand until you can grasp the hand-hold on the end of the boom, or the uphaul close to it. You have two hands and two feet: the *mast hand* is the one which will, when you are sailing, be closest to the mast, as will the *mast foot*; the *sail hand* is the hand nearest the centre of the sail as is the *sail foot*.

4. The weight of the rig and the drag of any wind in it is enough to support you pulling in the reverse direction. Your feet should be, at this time, either side of the mast step.

5. Step further back with the sail foot until it is over the daggerboard casing and at the same time, keeping hold of the uphaul with your sail hand, cross your mast hand over and grasp the boom.

6. Draw the boom forward across your body and, letting go of the uphaul, grasp the boom so that both hands are shoulder width apart. Bringing the boom forward will prevent the board shooting up into wind as you gently pull in with your sail hand. Reposition your mast foot so that it is just behind the mast step. You should now be sailing forwards.

THE WAY THE BOARD STEERS
The technique of sailing a board is very different from sailing a dinghy. In a dinghy, where the mast goes the boat goes too, but with a board the mast has a universal

WHEN YOU FIRST SAIL A BOARD

Make sure the board is a high-volume board that has plenty of buoyancy.

Use a small area sail.

Find somewhere where, or some time when, there are no waves.

Choose a wind that is not too light nor too strong – 5 to 10 knots is about right.

Wear at least the long-john bottom of a wet-suit.

Do not venture far from shore and remember that on-shore wind directions are the easiest for learning.

If you get into difficulty drop the rig and sit it out – do not, whatever you do, try to swim back to shore.

Fig. 1.3 The parts of a sailboard

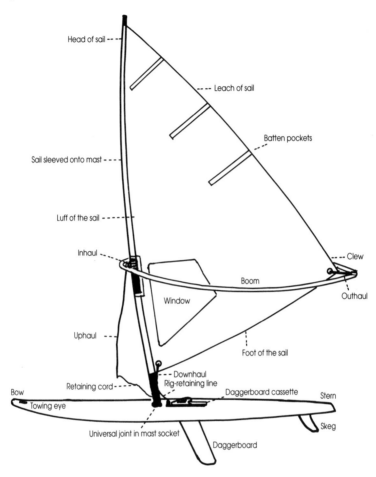

joint that means it can be moved anywhere. That is important because you have no rudder on a board and have to use your sail as a rudder. You need to understand this before you start or it may well be a long, wet time before the penny drops.

Cut out a bit of stiff card to represent the board and mark on it the relative positions of mast-step and daggerboard cassette. Mount it on a flat bit of wood with a drawing pin through the daggerboard cassette. This simulates the board turning about its daggerboard position. The force on the sail must be thought of as two arrows (see Fig. 1.4(a)):

- a driving force arrow straight forwards, and
- a sail force arrow perpendicularly sideways.

Fig. 1.4 (a) The force developed by the sail can be replaced by two forces – a sideways (or heeling) force and a force forward that provides way
(b) Understanding how to steer a board away from the wind
(c) Understanding how to steer a board towards the wind

(a)

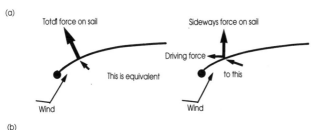

(b)

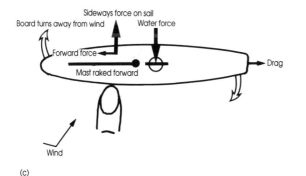

(c)

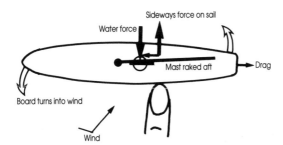

If the board is to sail forwards and not crab sideways (make leeway) the sail force has to be counterbalanced by a water force on the sides of the daggerboard, skeg and board as the wind tries to push the board to leeward. This water force acts around the position of the daggerboard cassette.

On your model simulator use your finger (see Fig. 1.4(b)) to represent the sail force and imagine swinging the mast forwards over its step. The sail force acting somewhere forward of the centre of the sail moves forward too and, as you simulate it with your finger, the board swings away from the wind. Similarly if you swing the mast back over the stern of the board the sail force moves back behind the water force and the board turns into the wind. Again as in Fig. 1.4(c) your finger, representing the moveable sail force, shows what happens.

The board sails straight forward when the sail force and the water force are in the same line. So you steer by constantly swinging the sail backwards and forwards.

FIRST LEGS

It helps a great deal to know where the wind is coming from and where you ought to be sailing towards. Adopt the technique described for directing the board compared to the wind on page 4. It is best to sail across the wind at first, and here is where the start of a seabreeze is so useful for boardsailing beginners.

The seabreeze blows more or less straight on-shore. You can therefore sail along the shoreline in relatively shallow water so that when you find you cannot get the board to come about you will not be miles out on the open ocean, but can jump off and turn round. Of course, on restricted inland waters you have different problems like tumbling off into soft mud in creeks and estuaries. The on-shore breeze also means that even if you cannot do anything else, the wind will blow you into shore.

Side-shore winds, so beloved by more experienced boardsailors, are not good for the newcomer. If the wind blows off-shore is there some nearby stretch of inland water you could go to rather than risk being blown out to sea and having to be rescued?

TURNING ROUND

A board is not a very responsive craft when it comes to making alterations to your course, and you will very often have problems coming about. In a light wind it is often easier to gybe (turn round away from the wind) than to tack. To gybe you:

1. tilt the rig forwards and towards the wind. This pushes the bow away from the wind. As the wind comes behind you, balance on the centre of the board. Then

2. let go with your sail hand and let the rig swing forwards over the bow

3. grab the uphaul with your sail hand

4. move round the mast step to the new windward side and pull the rig forwards with your sail hand as you grab the boom with your mast hand

5. reposition your hands as you sheet in on the new leg.

Allow plenty of room inshore of you to complete this manoeuvre until you become experienced. To tack you:

1. tilt the rig backwards to bring the board into the wind and keep it tilted back as you
2. grasp the uphaul, having moved your feet either side of the mast
3. shuffle round to the new windward side as the board comes onto the wind
4. grasp the boom with your mast hand and bring the rig forwards towards the sailing position as you reposition your feet for sailing the new leg and
5. grasp the boom with your sail hand and adjust your position for the new leg.

You will be forced to come about this way if you sail close along the shore with an on-shore breeze unless the beach shelves very slowly.

RUNNING BEFORE THE WIND
This is the most difficult of all boardsailing techniques for the beginner. There is nothing to support you as there is when you have a sail force to lean against on other points of sailing. If you are prone to fall off then certainly you will fall off when running before the wind, especially if you have sailed a dinghy and habitually kick the daggerboard up to reduce friction when you turn off the wind. Keep the daggerboard down in light winds when running – it stabilises an otherwise hairy ride.

MORE ADVANCED SAILING
In the above short notes you will have just enough to enable you to sail a board and turn it round. When you have left the 'always tumbling off' stage behind then get a book so that you can refine your techniques and maybe learn some of the more advanced ways of starting – like water starts – as well as other board wrinkles.

SELF RESCUE
If you do get into a situation where you cannot get back to shore drop your rig at once. Release the mast from its step and drag the rig over you as you sit astride the board. Remove any battens and roll up the sail, having released the outhaul and the inhaul. Lay boom and mast centrally down the board and, lying face downwards over them, paddle your way back to shore. You need energy for this so always sail well within your capabilities. If you must have help from the shore use the recognised signals for distress, which are:

Help required: Clench your fist and wave your raised arm above your head bending it at the elbow.

No help required: Make an 'O' for OK with thumb and index finger, arm should be vertical and held still until acknowledged.

Small smoke flares and/or a whistle should be carried if conditions are likely to get a bit rough.

Apparent wind

The wind you feel in any sailing craft that is not running before the wind is the apparent wind. The apparent wind is always from a direction nearer the bow than the true wind (see Fig. 1.5(a)).

When beating to windward the apparent wind is only ahead of the true wind by between 10° and 5°. So if you want to estimate where the true wind is coming from look at the masthead flag or pennant and mentally rotate about 10° towards the beam of the craft (see Fig. 1.5(b)). The faster the craft is sailing the smaller the angle.

Turn off the wind by about 15° so as to be close reaching and the angle between apparent and true winds increases to 30° in light winds and 20° in strong ones (see Fig. 1.5(c)).

When beam reaching in strong winds the angles do not increase much from the value when close reaching, but in light winds the angle may be as much as 40° between apparent and true winds (see Fig. 1.5(d)). Thus to know if you really are beam reaching you must have the masthead flag or pennant showing the apparent wind from about 45° on the bow.

Fig. 1.5 How adding the craft's forward way into the wind produces an apparent wind

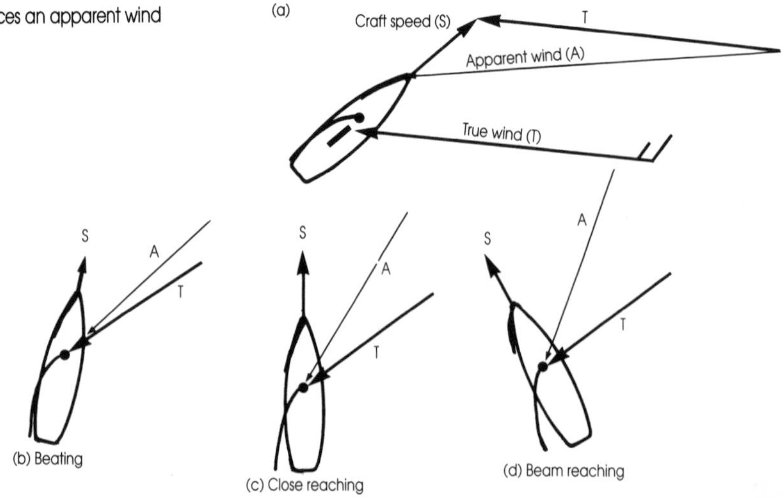

(a) Craft speed (S)   T
Apparent wind (A)
True wind (T)

(b) Beating

(c) Close reaching

(d) Beam reaching

The land has a tremendous effect on the speed of the wind, lowering it by some two-thirds from its speed, say, two thousand feet up. Forecasters measure the 2,000 feet wind from the distance apart of the isobars on their weather maps. As an example, let us say they find that over your locality at a particular time the 2,000 feet wind (called the 'gradient' wind) is about 20 knots. The wind over the open sea is taken to be two-thirds of the gradient, i.e. about 15 knots, and the wind over the land to be about a half of that over the sea, or around 7 knots. These figures are a guide and they appear on TV charts together with a rough idea of the direction (see Fig. 2.1). Thus waters that are sheltered by the land will have relatively low wind speeds compared with the same wind that has travelled a long way over the sea. Then fairly nice conditions may become difficult, especially as waves will be that much bigger (see Fig. 2.2).

It is a great help to have made some reasonable estimate of the wind where you intend to sail, from observations made at home; this is covered in the next section. Table 2.1 shows how to get an idea of what Beaufort force the wind is wherever you are.

How strong will the wind be?

If you know what the wind is doing ashore, how do you find out what sail to use when you get down to the water? We shall have to split the remarks in two. Open shores looking out into the open sea will be considered *large waters*, while inside

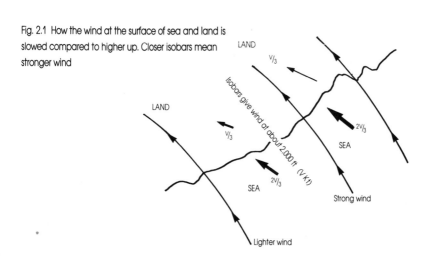

Fig. 2.1 How the wind at the surface of sea and land is slowed compared to higher up. Closer isobars mean stronger wind

LAND

LAND

Isobars give wind at about 2,000 ft (V kt)

$^V/_3$

$^V/_3$

$2^V/_3$

$2^V/_3$

SEA

SEA

Strong wind

Lighter wind

TABLE 2.1 THE SCALE OF WIND SPEED FOR DINGHIES AND BOARDS

Beaufort No. & symbol	General description	Limit of mean speed (knots)	Wind symbols used on charts	Land signs	Dinghy criteria	Board criteria	State of sea
0	Calm	Less than 1		Calm Smoke rises vertically. Leaves do not stir.	Sails will not fill. Racing flag will not respond. Flies and tell-tales just respond.	Stand there and hope for some wind.	Sea mirror-smooth. Calm enough to preserve shape of reflections of sails, masts etc.
1	Light air	1-3		1-2 kt Smoke drifts. Wind vanes do not respond.	Sails fill. Racing flags may not be reliable. Flies and tell-tales respond. Crew and helmsman on opposite sides of the craft.	Six square metre sails fill and board begins to make steady speed.	Scaly or shell-shaped ripples. No foam crests to be seen on open sea.
2	Light breeze	4-6		3-7 Wind felt on face. Leaves rustle. Light flags not extended. Wind vanes respond.	Useful way can be made. Racing flag reliable. Helmsman and crew sit to windward.	Power developed in sail. Board accelerates smoothly. No need to hike out yet.	Small short wavelets with glassy crests that do not break.
3	Gentle breeze	7-10		8-12 Light flags extended. Leaves in constant motion.	Helsman and crew sit on weather gunwale. Spinnakers fill. Fourteen-footers and above may plane.	Easy sailing on all points. Board planing on a reach. Lightweights hike out.	Large wavelets. Crests may break but foam is of glassy appearance. A few scattered white horses may be seen when wind at upper limit.
4	Moderate breeze	11-16		13-17 Most flags extend fully. Small branches move. Dust and loose paper may be raised.	Dinghy crews lie out. Twelve-foot dinghies may plane; longer dinghies will plane. The best general working breeze.	Nice conditions for those with any sort of experience. Too strong for beginners. In waves use 4.5 m² sail. Board now planing on all points but maybe not downwind. A harness is useful.	Small waves lengthen. Fairly frequent white horses.
5	Fresh breeze	17-21		18-22 Small trees in leaf sway. Tops of tall trees in noticeable motion.	Dinghies ease sheets in gusts. Crews use all weight to keep craft upright. Some capsizes.	Beginners need a small sail (4m²) especially in waves. Only heavy experienced sailors can use a full sized sail. Foot straps useful. Fast exciting sailing.	Moderate waves. Many white horses.
6	Strong breeze	22-27		23-27 Large branches in motion. Whistling heard in wires.	Dinghies overpowered when carrying full sail. Many capsizes. Crews find difficulty in holding craft upright even when spilling wind.	A wave-jumping wind but still need a reduced sail area (4m²). Heavy experienced sailors can use 5m² or even 6m² in sheltered waters. The board now really hums.	Large waves form and extensive foam crests are prevalent. Spray may be blown off some wave tops.

Near gale (American usage: Moderate gale)	28-33	Whole trees in motion. Inconvenience felt when walking against wind.	28-32	Sea heaps up and white foam from breaking waves begins to be blown in streaks along the wind direction.	Only for the very experienced and then in open water only with care. Small sail is a must.	Dinghies fully reefed. Difficult to sail even on main alone. This is the absolute top limit for dinghies – other than in *extremis*.
Gales (fresh gale)	34-40	Twigs broken off trees. Generally impedes progress on foot. Rarely experienced inland.	33-37	Moderately high waves of greater length. Edges of crests begin to break into spindrift. Foam blown in well-marked streaks along the wind.	A real expert might be out in sheltered waters pushing himself and his board to the limits.	Dinghies may survive if expertly handled in the seaway on foresail alone.
8			38-42			

harbour mouths, coastal lagoons, etangs, creeks, rivers, lakes and reservoirs are *small waters*.

The great effect of the land on cutting down the wind speed means that the speed will not pick up properly within a mile or two of the shore when it blows out onto open water. Most small waters will therefore be more or less sheltered, but when the wind blows directly along a long straight waterway it can gain as much speed as if it were on the open sea. Only you can assess things like that because no book can allow for all combinations of wind direction, waterway direction and speed. (See Fig. 2.3.)

CASE 1 OFF-SHORE WINDS

Land wind speeds shown in Table 2.2 are either assessed by you, given by a met office or a weather forecast, and are relevant for large waters (up to a mile or two out) when the wind is blowing off the land or for small waters.

If the wind blows from the shore make sure there is someone about to send help if you get into difficulties. If the wind blows side-shore from some distance away (i.e. a few miles perhaps) expect more open-sea conditions. Waves should not be a problem in most cases, but this does not apply to harbour entrances and similar situations (see page 62).

CASE 2 ON-SHORE WINDS

Land wind speeds shown in Table 2.3 are either assessed by you, given by a met office, coastguard or weather forecast, and are relevant for large waters when the wind is blowing on-shore. The wave heights given are on the assumptions that the wind has blown for some 4 to 6 hours from the same direction, and that the water is deep enough to avoid the steepening effects of a shelving shore. They will be much bigger inshore. The sail sizes take account of wave conditions and allow for the majority of gusts.

Fig. 2.2 How the land affects the wind. Wherever the wind can break free of the land it increases and where it blows more or less parallel to narrow waterways it increases again

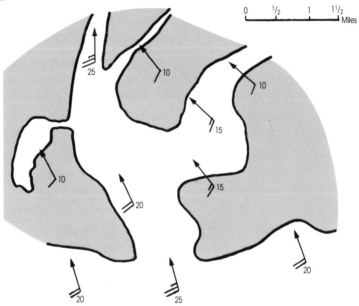

Fig. 2.3 A similar diagram to Fig. 2.2 but for off-shore winds. Winds that blow closely past the edges of the land increase their speed locally and may shift direction

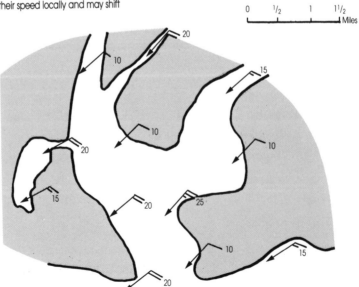

TABLE 2.2 OFF-SHORE WINDS

Land wind speed (knots)	Corresponding wind over sea (knots)	Suggested sail m²
10 14 16 } Force 4	12 Force 4	5.5–6.5
	18 21 } Force 5	4.5–6.5
18 20 } Force 5	25 28 } Force 6	4.0–5.5
22 24 26 } Force 6	33 Force 7	3.5–5.0
	38 42 } Force 8	3.5–4.5 (but may be too much)
28 30 32 } Force 7	Too strong	

TABLE 2.3 ON-SHORE WINDS

Land wind speed (knots)	Corresponding wind over shoreside waters (knots)	Suggested sail m²	Waves up to
10 14 16 } Force 4	11 16 } Force 4	4.5–6.0	5 ft
	19 Force 5	4.0–5.5	8 ft
18 20 } Force 5	24 28 } Force 6	3.5–5.0	11 ft
	31 32 } Force 7	3.5–4.0	16 ft
22 24 26 } Force 6			
	34 36 } Force 8	3.5–4.0	22 ft
28 30 32 } Force 7			

The wind will be stronger away from the beach when:

winds blow from land to sea

winds blow along a high coast

winds blow through narrow waterways.

There is less difference between land and sea:

during the afternoon compared with morning or evening

when the wind blows on-shore.

Estimating wind speed

To make a reliable estimate of the likely wind speed on whatever shore you sail is not easy. Yet while still at home it helps to know the rough speed so you can take the correct sails, boom, etc., and – if you do not want to bother should it be too strong – whether even to set out.

The wind will be at its strongest under the following conditions:

when it blows straight in off the sea

when it blows parallel to a narrow waterway

when it blows into a narrowing estuary

when big shower clouds (cumulus and cumulo-nimbus) are about or are growing around the sky.

You have to relate your home estimate to these factors using the tables on page 19 as a guide.

At home, to get a reliable wind, you need:

1. a clear space like a field or a park where the obstructions upwind are far enough away to fit roughly the height of the top half of your thumb held at arm's length as explained on page 41;

2. a little time to watch the antics of the tops of trees, the way flags are extended or the wind vane on the church is acting.

The 'land signs' of the Beaufort scale suggest using:

Smoke for Force 0 since it rises vertically and in Force 1 it drifts. After that smoke does not help.

Wind vanes, which at Force 1 do not respond (although masthead vanes on yachts or racing flags on dinghies will) but at Force 2 begin to move. After that they only indicate direction and nothing about speed.

Trees whose leaves rustle in a light breeze of Force 2. The leaves are in constant motion in Force 3, but branches are not. Small branches move in Force 4 and there will be obvious motion in the topmost parts of tall trees when it is Force 4 to 5. At Force 5 small trees in leaf sway and at Force 6 large branches move while there is whistling in overhead wires. Whole trees sway in Force 7 and at Force 8 (gale) they begin to lose exposed twigs.

Flags Light flags are not extended at Force 2 but they are at Force 3. Force 4 will extend most flags and at Force 5 they will be hard out and looking like the rigid ones used by the astronauts on the moon. Often flags are to be seen on tall buildings but then it must be remembered that the related surface wind speed may be a Beaufort Force lower than that indicated by the flag.

Estimating wind direction

This is often easier than estimating wind speed. Wind vanes and weather cocks on churches are usually reliable as are flags on tall buildings. What are not reliable are bunting flags etc. that are often used for advertising by garage forecourts, or any low-sited wind vane around buildings. The best and most reliable arrow for the true wind direction lies in the direction of drift of low clouds like cumulus. The wind you get this way is the 'gradient' wind and is not affected by the mass of obstacles on the ground. It is also useful to remember that the gradient wind direction is the same as that of the 'tramlines' of the isobars on a weather map. So if you find the wind direction from sight of a weather chart on TV then the low clouds should be moving the same way.

Finding the gradient wind from observing low clouds

1. Face the direction the clouds are coming from.
2. Look to both sides to ensure you are really facing the true direction.

Having found the wind at cloud level is, say, SW you can find the wind direction at the surface (which is slightly different) by looking 15° to the left if your sailing wind will be coming over the sea, or 30° to the left if it will be coming over the land. You can estimate the former 15° using the same yardstick as given on page 41 for finding the zone of least wind, however, this time using it horizontally: hold thumb and first finger outstretched at arm's length and that gap subtends about 15°; double it for 30°.

If you can get used to this method (and of course you have to have some low clouds to do it) it is the most reliable way of finding the true wind direction wherever you are. The only time it might break down is when mountains begin to get as high as the clouds, but otherwise it is a universal way of finding the true sailing wind. It is worth remembering that in the evening and in the morning, when winds are at their lightest, the 30° angle mentioned above could well need to be increased to 45°.

What if the surface wind is entirely different?

Let us assume you intend to go sailing one afternoon. You go out and watch the way the cumulus clouds are moving and find they are coming from a certain direction. Every other sign points to the wind you feel being from some other, possibly almost diametrically opposite, direction. You then know you have a local wind.

If you are not too many miles from the sea coast this will be a seabreeze and the clouds could show the wind above the breeze to be from some point inland while the surface wind will be from the direction of the coast.

If in a hilly area this wind could well be a local wind draining off the higher ground or channelled by a local valley or by the waterway itself. Near the coast in the early morning it could be the last of a night wind that has blown from land to sea and is not destined to last long.

These will all be light or gentle winds, but what if the wind is stronger and the wind at cloud level is very different from what you have at ground level? Then you look around for signs of a local depression. There are little lows that run along fronts (especially cold fronts) and which never develop into full-blown depressions. They are called waves (the reason for that is evident from Fig. 2.4). The local wind will blow straight into the centre of the wave as it reaches you, but the wind at cloud level may not follow. Thus we get contrary winds. The same goes for fronts. If an angry wall of cloud bears down on you and it is obvious that the wind at cloud level is considerably different in direction from the wind you feel, then expect immediate strong squalls. They may not last long, but they can be upsetting while they last.

The wind at cloud level and at the surface may be different because:	a mountain or valley wind is blowing
a seabreeze is blowing	a local depression centre is passing
a land breeze is blowing	a sharp front is passing

Fig. 2.4 What happens when a small wave depression ripples by. The weather often does not clear very quickly

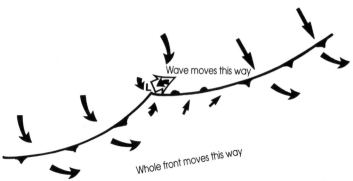
Wave moves this way

Whole front moves this way

Allowing for gusts

There is a big problem with choosing a sail size for a board or a crew size for a dinghy and that concerns the way the wind behaves. The wind speeds you estimate from the previous sections, or which are given in forecasts, are average speeds whereas the wind is always gusting above its average and sinking (lulling) by the same margin below the average. Now the latter does not matter, but the former does. Table 2.4 shows what the highest speed will be when the average wind speed is given in knots (or assessed from Beaufort criteria).

TABLE 2.4 GUST SPEEDS

Mean wind speed (Kt)	Beaufort force	Average gust speed (Kt)	Equivalent sail area (m²)	Maximum gust speed (Kt)	Equivalent sail area (m²)
8	3 Gentle breeze	14 (Moderate)	5.5	20 (Fresh)	4.5
14	4 Moderate breeze	25 (Strong)	4.5	30 (Near gale)	4.0
18	5 Fresh breeze	28 (Strong)	4.5	36 (Gale)	3.5
24	6 Strong breeze	36 (Gale)	3.5	44 (Strong gale)	3.5

These figures tend to paint too gloomy a picture because the gusts only reach the maximum speed now and again. The sail areas given are those which you would need if you did not spill wind during the stronger puffs. The following rules may help:

1. Gusts get much stronger than the average wind speed when big cumulus clouds are about and especially when showers occur.

2. Gusts are muted in the early mornings, evenings and when layer clouds cover the sailing venue.

3. There is less noticeable difference between average speed and gust speeds in the afternoon, but this is because the average speed has risen as well.

4. Maximum gust speeds will be encountered on rare occasions in association with fronts, showers and thunderstorms. If you meet a monster gust just drop your sail and sit it out; it cannot last too long.

Seeing gusts coming

There are various ways in which the tell-tale signs of approaching gusts can be appreciated. They include:

1. Boats upwind careening to the sudden increase in wind.

2. The 'splash' marks of the gust's leading edge coming across the water.

3. The sign of rain 'curtains' below dark-based shower clouds. The gusts will come with, or ahead of, the rain.

4. Gusts often appear under the leading edges of individual cumulus clouds and the clouds themselves will show where there is likely to be a gust.

Sailing a dinghy out from a shore

First ascertain how the wind is blowing compared with the shore. There are three main directions:

1. you are on a lee shore – the wind is blowing directly off the water;

2. you are on a weather shore – the wind is blowing directly off the shore;

3. the wind is side-shore.

ON A LEE SHORE

There are two main things to contend with:

- the wind will try continually to blow you back to shore;
- the waves will try to cast you back to shore.

Either way you have to know techniques for getting afloat and clear of the shoreside breakers.

In Fig. 3.1 we illustrate the technique for getting off a lee shore:

1. The crew (C) wades out and holds the dinghy head to wind, but stands on the side away from the direction the helmsman (H) intends to go. It is to the right in this example. The helmsman crouches in the centre of the boat under the flogging boom and lowers the centreboard as far as possible.

2. The crew pulls the boat forward and at the same time pushes it away from the shore while scrambling aboard. Both crew and helmsman man the weather side ready to sit the boat up as required.

3. As the dinghy cannot sail into the wind at angles in the 'no-go' zone, the helmsman will bear away using the foresail to push the bows off the wind until the mainsail is fully drawing. The centreboard must be fully down by now.

On-shore winds create large waves – and the wind does not have to be strong to do so. A gently shelving beach will heap up the incoming waves into breakers with which the dinghy crew must launch in phase. Wait until a wave is about to pass under the dinghy. Then push off as rapidly as possible and try to get the sails drawing before the next wave strikes. Get onto a fast close reach in order to burst through the waves and avoid being thrown back towards the shore. If the waves are very big then the crew will have to get very wet towing the boat out to beyond the shore breakers (still assuming that the beach shelves slowly). If the beach shelves rapidly the crew may have to stand in the water close by the sailing position and push the boat away while scrambling in. The centreboard can go down at once so making the boat point well and making it easier to punch the incoming waves.

ON A WEATHER SHORE

Waves are not usually a problem on a weather shore, but you cannot sail out bow first unless the wind is light. In Fig. 3.2 two techniques are illustrated.

1. The crew holds the boat head to wind by standing beside it. The helmsman sorts out the sheets and holds the tiller towards the side they wish to sail – in this case to the right along the shore or on starboard tack.

2. The crew scrambles in and the helmsman makes a 'sternboard', i.e. he drifts back and the reversed rudder pushes the stern away from the sailing direction. The centreboard is fully lowered.

Fig. 3.1 Sailing a dinghy off a shore with an on-shore wind

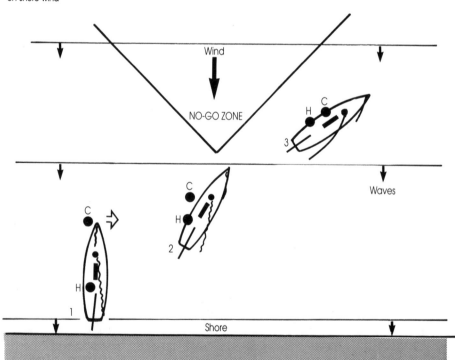

3. As soon as practicable helmsman and crew harden in and get sailing, but use the way created to

4. Bear away onto a broad reach away from the shore. It does not matter whether this is a shelving or steep-to shore, the technique is the same.

The alternative is:

5. The crew holds the boat across the wind with the sails flogging.

6. The crew scrambles in and immediately hauls in the foresail so that the dinghy bears away rapidly seaward. The helmsman prepares for what may well be an almost instantaneous plane.

WITH A SIDE-SHORE WIND
Here you can use either of two techniques. There will be waves to contend with very often. In the first method:

Fig. 3.2 Sailing a dinghy off a shore with an off-shore wind. The waves will be the result of swell left over from previous wind

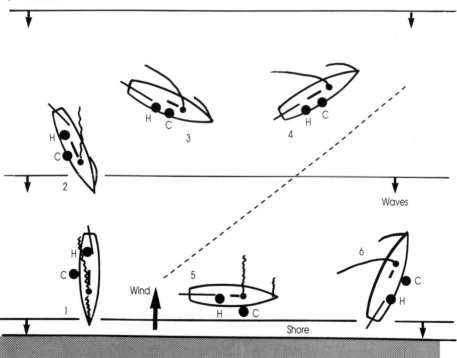

1. The crew holds the dinghy across the wind with sails flogging.

2. The crew jumps in and both crew and helmsman harden in somewhat and allow for an immediate plane. The centreboard needs to be half down.

In the second method:

3. The crew holds the dinghy head to wind. The centreboard is lowered as far as possible.

4. The crew pushes off and scrambles in to harden in the foresail so that the dinghy bears away and both crew and helmsman

5. Allow for a beat by ensuring that the centreboard is fully down at the first available opportunity.

In practice it is unusual for the wind to be blowing either directly on-shore, off-shore or side-shore. It will most often be at some oblique angle in which case the wind direction compared with the shoreline will dictate the tack on which you will set off.

Bringing a dinghy back to shore

Here the lee shore is much more of a problem than the weather shore, and the side-shore is a different, but usually much easier, problem.

LEE SHORE
Assuming the wind is blowing directly on-shore and is not strong so that the waves are not large (a seabreeze afternoon for example), then proceed as in Fig. 3.3:

1. Sail in on a broad reach with very little centreboard.

2. (a) Round up into wind so that boat drifts back towards the shore.
(b) The helmsman can leap out, being in the shallowest water, while the crew, being nearest to the halyard cleats, lowers the sails.

If the shore is steep-to and/or there are large waves then you have to get ashore quickly. So:

3. Ride the boat into the shore and when the centreboard grounds both crew and helmsman leap out and check the way. The crew can move forward and haul the boat head to wind. If you can lower the mainsail before beaching all well and good. However, do not lower all sail as you need the forward way to combat the undertow of the receding waves. In the latter case let fly the foresail at the moment of grounding and manhandle the boat ashore.

WEATHER SHORE

Assuming the wind is blowing directly off-shore you can sail in close-hauled on either tack and:

1. When the centreboard grounds push the boat into the wind while

2. The crew jumps in to steady the boat and check excess way or prevent the boat being blown back out to sea.

If the wind is at an angle to the shore then the tack to come in on is the one which is more parallel to the shore so that:

3. You keep the centreboard down as long as possible before

4. Turning onto the shore head to wind.

Assessing the state of the shore

There are some fine sands along the Sussex coast of England – and some fine weather too which is why this coast is dubbed the English Riviera. However, at low water spring tides sizeable rocks are revealed in many places. At states of the tide

Fig. 3.3 Running a dinghy into shore with an on-shore wind

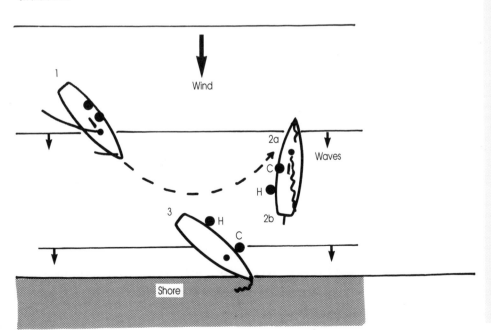

either side of low water, as well as at low water neaps, these rocks do not break surface, but they can cause some nasty accidents if dinghy or boardsailors jump out or fall off onto them. This example shows that you must not assume that because a beach is sandy and gently shelving that it will have no hidden dangers. Not every groyne will have a marker on it to show how far it extends seawards so that near high water, if sailing close to the shore, there are potential dangers lurking close to many beaches. On this same bit of coast there is a submerged forest off Selsey Bill and the boles of the trees present another form of hazard at low water.

There may be sizeable holes in an otherwise flat stretch of beach which are quite invisible until you disappear into one. Where a little stream runs down the beach into the sea may seem a wonderful place to run into to land but allow for soft sand or mud on the edges of such rithes. If you land on a muddy shore, remember that matt-looking mud surfaces are usually hard while smooth and glossy ones are often soft. Anywhere close to reeds or grass will be firmer than elsewhere.

If you arrive at a sailing venue and it is not low water when you first take a look at the beach, do not take what you see as a sure sign of what the beach is like. Either ask the locals or take the trouble to inspect the low-water line for hidden dangers.

Sailing a board off a sandy shore

So long as the wind is not too strong and the waves are relatively small then proceed as in Fig. 3.4. With a side-shore wind walk the board into the water.

1. One hand holds the stern up as the bow is pushed down the beach. The other hand supports the rig with the sail flogging.

2. On getting into the water push a little of the daggerboard down and holding onto the boom with both hands harden in somewhat with the sail hand (the other hand nearest the mast is the mast hand) and allow the force in the sail to help you climb aboard.

3. Whenever you launch from a beach get sailing as soon as you can as even quite small waves may continually tip you off. Also remember that you need a smaller rig as the wind speed increases and especially as the waves get bigger.

IF THERE ARE WAVES

Proceed as in Fig. 3.4 and push the board into the water on its edge.

1. With one hand under the skeg and some of the daggerboard down use the other hand to support the rig and do not let it fall into the water. If it is impossible to hold it up in this wind then go for a smaller rig.

2. As soon as you are through one wave climb aboard as rapidly as possible and harden in the sail.

3. Sail as quickly as possible through the next wave. Stay on a reach until clear of the shoreside breakers.

A more advanced technique is to push the board into deep water:

4. Pull the sail over to windward and let the force of the wind lift you up onto the board using your feet as a fulcrum. This is called a water start and is only practicable with winds that are moderate or above and after some practice. It may be the only way of getting started when the wind is directly on-shore and the waves are sizeable.

Beginners and improvers will find it best to develop confidence on inland waters before ever braving the waves. However, the mornings of seabreeze days are good times for beginners as there is often about ten knots of wind from seaward, but the sea remains relatively calm. Under the same wind strength there will be much larger waves by afternoon.

OFF-SHORE WIND – WINDWARD SHORE

As the board is such an unstable craft when sailing before the wind, sailing one straight off a beach with anything greater than a gentle wind may present a

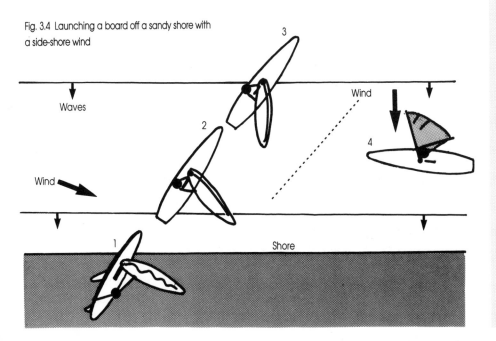

Fig. 3.4 Launching a board off a sandy shore with a side-shore wind

problem. The basic rule is that the sail must be flogging in the wind and the board must be at right angles to it (as in 1 of Fig. 3.4), so the board must be walked into relatively deep water. The daggerboard must be down. You climb onto the board at the same time as sheeting in with the sail hand and sail side-shore until you have settled down and can bear away for deeper water. Despite the off-shore wind there can sometimes be waves which make for a more difficult start.

SHINGLE OR ROCKY SHORES

These present a real problem at the launching stage. The board will be scraped and gouged by the pebbles and/or rocks if it is pushed into the water using the techniques described above. In this case the board must be carried into the water and rigged there. With the board across the wind and the sail laid on the water away from the wind you gain hold of the boom by using the uphaul. Then grab the boom with the mast hand and quickly follow that with the sail hand so that you can sail off across the wind.

This is not a book about sailing technique, so only the briefest advice is offered as to how to sail. There are many texts on the techniques of sailing dinghies and boards. In the end the best way is to get someone who knows to help you learn to sail a dinghy, and go to a reputable school to learn the rudiments of boardsailing.

4 A DAY'S WIND

What the wind will do during the course of a fair sailing day depends on where you are and how hard the wind blows. In what follows you will be given hints on the things that are likely to happen depending on the time of day and the strength and direction of the wind compared with the shores you are sailing from. The basic principles are:

1. The wind will get up in the morning, increase in the afternoon and then decrease into the evening (Fig. 4.1).

2. Seabreezes will blow over the coastal belt if conditions are right for them.

3. Seabreezes usually start late morning and blow through into the late afternoon or early evening.

The reason why the wind 'goes to bed' in the evening and gets up in the morning lies in the formation of what is called a 'temperature inversion', or simply an inversion. It is normal for the air temperature to drop as we ascend, but most nights the air above the surface is warmer than where we are. This is because the wind during the day has created eddies that have transported the heat of the earth up to higher levels. As night approaches the land cools and extracts heat from the surface air. So cold air now lies under warmer air and an inversion is present. This inversion acts like an invisible 'lid' and locks the wind away above itself leaving the surface wind to die through colliding with surface obstacles. So the wind goes down overnight.

In the morning the sun creates thermals which punch through the inversion and break it up (Fig. 4.2). The upper wind finds its way onto the surface and speeds up the previously sluggish morning wind. So the day's wind starts to blow. It gets stronger in the afternoon and then begins to weaken as the inversion process starts again.

Fig. 4.1 The way the speed of the wind picks up to become maximum in the early afternoon on a normal day

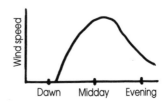

Fig. 4.2 How wind appears in the morning as the sun
on the land breaks the overnight inversion

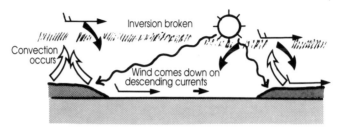

Large waters

Table 4.1 gives probable wind developments on seaside beaches under the following
conditions:

Day with light or gentle morning wind Gentle means that the wind is less than 10
knots at breakfast time. It is almost 10 knots if tree leaves move constantly in the

TABLE 4.1 WIND CONDITIONS FOR LARGE WATERS

Wind	Breakfast period 0700–0900 (LST)	Morning period 0900–1200 (LST)	Afternoon period 1200–1600 (LST)	Evening 1600–Dusk (LST)
Off-shore	Sea smooth. Wind blows light to gentle from inland onto the sea. Any cloud usually breaks to give a sunny morning.	Wind increases but later falters and then reverses to blow on-shore as a seabreeze. This happens when breakfast wind is light. Sea slight at first but waves will become larger as the day progresses. Fluffy lumps of cumulus cloud grow around the sky. If they do not, the seabreeze may blow very sluggishly.	Wind may have blown off-shore for most of the morning but then begins to drop away before reversing, often with maddening shifts of strength and direction. This follows a gentle breakfast wind. Sea remains slight. If seabreeze blows then it becomes blazingly sunny over beaches and inshore waters.	Any seabreeze will die away often to calm. Otherwise wind blows back from land to sea.
On-shore	Sea slight but shore can induce waves that are difficult to launch through. Sunny or partly cloudy. (This section does not deal with cloudy conditions.)	Wind increases and waves begin to grow towards moderate. Sunshine helps the strength of a breakfast on-shore wind. If wind does not increase much with the morning then it often gets very hot.	Wind may grow to moderate breeze and white horses sparkle in the sunshine. A great sailing afternoon. If cloud increases into this period wind may do anything.	Wind goes down but waves are still sizeable. Could be difficult sailing for boards.
Side-shore	If wind less than gentle and fair conditions, expect the seabreeze force to pull the wind round off the sea later.	Wind takes an angle on-shore on sunny or fair days. Cloud that grows over the land may not do so over the sea – or vice versa. If seabreeze force turns wind more nearly on-shore then it is usually under brilliant sunshine.	Wind will normally increase (and on-shore seabreeze certainly will) with corresponding gain in wave height.	Wind should go back to earlier direction but maybe it will come from a new direction.

breeze and a light flag or burgee is extended. If leaves rustle but light flags stay limp it is about 5 knots and the wind is a light breeze.

Time of day LST = local sun time.

Small waters

Table 4.2 gives probable wind developments on creeks, estuaries and rivers, etc., within ten miles of the main coastline under the following conditions:

Day with light or gentle morning wind The meaning of light and gentle is given in the previous section. These tables mainly refer to pleasant sailing days with light morning winds.

Time of day LST = local sun time.

TABLE 4.2 WIND CONDITIONS FOR SMALL WATERS

Wind	Breakfast period 0700–0900 (LST)	Morning period 0900–1200 (LST)	Afternoon period 1200–1600 (LST)	Evening 1600–Dusk (LST)
From inland or more nearly parallel to main sea coast	Light to calm with a tendency to blow along the waterway from inland.	Wind gets up as cloud appears. Wind is often variable at this time of day. Seabreeze may set in before end of period if 3–4 miles from main coast, preceded by a short calm period.	If sunshine, or sun and cloud, seabreeze should blow from main sea coast but a gentle breakfast wind could keep it out until the afternoon. Could be some wild wind shifts. Sometimes wind will go down by afternoon and even go calm, if you are around 10 miles inland.	If there has been a seabreeze it will often go calm but expect wind to come back from inland later (if you haven't already got it).
From direction of main sea coast	Light or gentle winds may be accompanied by cloudy conditions that break up later. If it stays cloudy expect only small increase in wind speed (unless forecast has said otherwise).	Wind will increase as morning progresses so that you may have a moderate wind by late morning. Can be gusty and there might be some showers.	Wind speed at maximum if sunny or partly cloudy. If still cloudy not much increase on the morning wind. Gusts might be up to 20 Kt even if breakfast wind was gentle.	Expect wind to go down but not to go calm as it can when the wind is from the direction of main sea coast.

GENERAL NOTES

These notes refer to days when it either starts sunny or becomes sunny to fair (less than half the sky covered in low clouds) later. The nearer you are to the main sea coast the more likely that the seabreeze will come in early. If the breakfast wind is moderate (tree branches move and most flags extend) do not expect a seabreeze, but its influence may decrease the wind in the afternoon when it should be at its strongest. Moderate winds off the sea in the morning mean planing conditions by the afternoon. If the forecast is for the fronts of a depression to come in during the day seabreezes are less likely, but winds are most likely to strengthen from a southerly point.

Inland waters

Table 4.3 gives likely wind developments on inland waters such as reservoirs and lakes more than ten miles from the main sea coast under these conditions:

Day with light or gentle breakfast-time winds   The meaning of light and gentle is given in an earlier section. This table refers to pleasant sailing days with not much low cloud at breakfast time.

Time of day   LST = local sun time.

TABLE 4.3   WIND CONDITIONS FOR INLAND WATERS

Wind	Breakfast period 0700–0900 (LST)	Morning period 0900–1200 (LST)	Afternoon period 1200–1600 (LST)	Evening 1600–Dusk (LST)
From inland or more nearly parallel to the main sea coast	Light to calm with a tendency to come from any local higher ground inland or down a local valley or along the waterway.	Wind gets up and blows more nearly in the direction as given by the forecast. However, wind still tries to follow narrow waterways. Cloud should increase but not so much as to completely hide the sun. Wind becomes quite gusty and variable very often. Chance of showers by end of period.	Wind at maximum. Strongest puffs ignore shape of the local terrain so may be very variable between gusts and lulls. Lightening wind in this period heralds seabreeze from the coast, but it may not get to you before late afternoon or early evening. Could produce impossibly light conditions or even go calm.	If wind has held up during the day expect it to remain or even increase. If calm or light airs induced by seabreeze, expect wind to come back from breakfast direction later unless forecast has given a new wind direction for this time. Calm can extend right through evening.
From directions towards the main sea coast	Generally a time of low wind speed. Cloud at this time in summer should break up later. Wind at this time could be sinking off local higher ground and funnelling through valleys or the waterway itself. If such a trend opposes the wind from seaward then could be calm for some time.	Wind will increase if sunny or fair. Could be moderate towards end of period. Elongated waterways could funnel wind and make it blow from directions not forecast. Could be very variable at this time of day.	Wind could be up to fresh even if breakfast wind was light, especially when wind blows more or less parallel to the waterway. Could be gusty even if average wind speed is not great.	Wind will decrease usually, but if it does not, seek a likely cause, i.e. forecast that says a depression is coming in.

GENERAL NOTES

You can expect conditions to be more cloudy inland than by the coast, and the further in from the main sea coast the less chance of problems with the seabreeze. The latter can sometimes run in 40–50 miles in late spring and early summer, but only arrive over rivers etc. that far inland sometime during the late evening. Expect the wind to be more variable inland than off the beach.

Length of the wind's day

Overnight calms that settle on coastlands and inland areas are 'woken up' by the sun shining on the land, but the sun needs to have risen about 30° above the horizon for it to begin to have a real effect. As the sun sinks, the land radiates more heat than it gains from the sun, the atmosphere stabilises and the wind begins to drop. Table 4.4 gives the GMT times when the sun is 30° or more above the horizon. Puffs of cumulus clouds appearing before these times show that the air is very unstable and likely to produce showers later.

TABLE 4.4 DATES AND TIMES AT WHICH SUN IS MORE THAN 30° ABOVE THE HORIZON

Latitude	Location	Dates	Feb 18 and Oct 25	Mar 21 and Sep 23	Apr 21 and Aug 23	June 22
58N	North Scotland, Skaggerak, North Baltic		Never higher than 20°	1030–1330	0830–1530	0700–1700
52N	Southern Ireland, Central Southern England, Holland,		Never higher than 27°	0930–1430	0800–1600	0700–1700
46N	Central Biscay coast of France, North Adriatic		1030–1330	0900–1500	0800–1800	0700–1700
38N	Lisbon, Toe of Italy, Southern Aegean		0930–1430	0830–1530	0800–1600	0700–1700

As seabreezes need sun on the land the table gives an indication of the earliest times we can expect seabreezes even when morning conditions are calm or light airs.

Length of day

You may want to sail early or sail late, or you might think of sailing from morning to night. So long as there is wind and the weather is good, why not? Table 4.5 gives in GMT the times of sunrise and sunset (to the nearest quarter of an hour) from 58N to 38N. The middle figure gives hours of daylight.

TABLE 4.5 DATES AND TIMES OF SUNRISE AND SUNSET

Latitude	Location	Dates	Feb 18 and Oct 25	Mar 21 and Sep 23	Apr 21 and Aug 23	June 22
58N	North Scotland, Skaggerak, North Baltic		0730–9–1630	0600–12–1800	0445–14½–1915	0300–18–2100
52N	Southern Ireland, Holland, Central Southern England, Poland		0700–10–1700	0600–12–1800	0500–14–1900	0345–16½–2015
46N	Central Biscay coast of France, North Adriatic		0656–10½–1715	0600–12–1800	0500–14–1900	0400–16–2000
38N	Lisbon, Toe of Italy, Southern Aegean		0630–11–1730	0600–12–1800	1515–13½–1845	0430–15–1930

At the end of winter and in the autumn the Mediterranean has a longer day than more northern climes. At the summer solstice (June 22) it will be light for three hours longer in the most northerly latitude than in the most southerly one.

5 WEATHER MAPS AND WIND

Weather maps are constantly to be seen on TV these days and something useful can be gained from them, even though the information is only on screen for a matter of seconds. The forecast chart for tomorrow can be an invaluable guide to what the wind will be like where you intend to sail because the isobars give the wind direction (see Fig. 5.1). There will be lows and highs enclosed by these isobars. The rules are:

Winds blow to keep *low* pressure on the left.

This means they blow to keep *high* pressure on the *right*.

Usually some wind arrows will be given during the forecast – sometimes on the weather map itself – which will confirm you have the correct direction. Suppose the isobars show the wind tomorrow to be due west. That will not be quite the wind you sail in. The surface wind is backed (shifted anticlockwise) from the direction shown by the isobars.

The angle of backing is:

About 15° over the sea or on coasts in winds with a long fetch.

About 30° over the land, but it can be more or less depending on the conditions.

Fig. 5.1 The features of the weather map

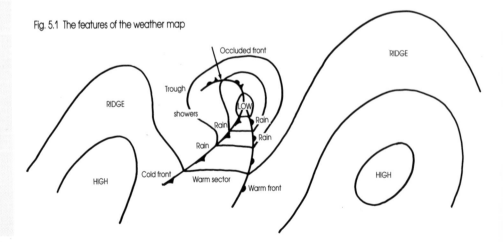

You have to draw in your mind an arrow flying along the isobaric tramlines and then rotate it anticlockwise through the above angles, depending on whether the coast will be facing the wind or the wind will be blowing from the land (see Fig. 2.1).

The distance between the isobars follows a rule:

$$\text{Distance apart} \times \text{Wind speed} = \text{Constant}$$

This means that should the distance between the isobars halve, the wind speed will double. Thus close isobars mean strong winds and widely spaced isobars mean light winds. You cannot gauge the exact wind speed just from looking at the map, but if you want to know what it will be you could video the forecast, freeze the forecast weather map and measure the distance apart using the technique I have described in my book *Reading the Weather* (published by Adlard Coles).

Gusts

What the isobars do tell you straight away is which way the big gusts in any variable airstream will come from. This is because sudden gusts are due to chunks of upper air brought down onto the surface by sinking convection currents (see Fig. 5.2). As they come from above and are not subjected to the earth's friction, they tend to come from the direction given by the isobars, which, as has been pointed out, is different from the surface wind direction.

When you sail inland waters then your wind will be that associated with the land and the variation between gusts and lulls in variable airstreams will be more noticeable than the corresponding wind on the coast. Very often in the mornings the difference in direction between gusts and lulls can be as much as 45° or more. This

Fig. 5.2 How unstable days produce a variable wind of gusts and lulls

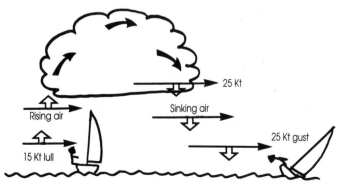

wide shift pattern will usually become less noticeable by the afternoon when the general wind speed increases.

Gust and lull patterns

When you get a fresh-feeling day with good visibility and cumulus clouds form, there will be a pattern of gusts and lulls (see Photo 2). The lowest parts of the wind speed pattern (lulls) will be followed by sudden increases (gusts) and then the wind will tend to stay up for as much as a few minutes before it begins to decrease in speed. Then after this gradual decrease into a lull the wind will suddenly gust again. The wind speed may almost double between lull and gust and, as the gust is wind from above brought down onto the surface, so it will veer (shift clockwise) in direction compared with the lull before it.

All winds will have a spectrum of shifts and speed variations, but often there is no discernible pattern as there is with a 'cumulus' airstream. We can, however, say:

- Lumpy skies mean lumpy winds.
- Featureless skies mean featureless winds.

Photo 2 Cumulus clouds mean a variable wind but often the weather is set fair when this kind of sky is seen.

As an example, on days with a complete layer of low cloud, while the wind will not be wholly steady, it will certainly be steadier than when big cumulus clouds dot the sky. As a further example, winds go 'flat' in the evenings when the cumulus clouds die out. Again the sky is featureless and so is the wind. It is the same in the mornings before the cumulus clouds develop.

Some airstreams are very variable indeed with a wide divergence in direction when they are blowing fastest and slowest. The wind direction is often easterly (or some point near there) when these big variations set in and the time is usually the morning. The speed is often not great with the highest puffs being only a matter of 10 knots or so, while the wind may sink to almost nothing in between. Winds need to be routed over land for the widest pattern of shifts.

Gusts and obstructions

Because of buildings and trees – in fact everything that gets in the way of the wind – the wind develops eddies. These go under the collective name of turbulence and the eddies get bigger as the wind speed increases. When turbulent eddies cross a sailing boat they produce little shifts that may only last a second or two. They are the 'noise' in the tune of the wind and they accompany the bigger gust–lull patterns described above. Expert sailors try to follow these little shifts if they can when beating to windward, but there is a bad side to them in that they tend to hamper recognition of the phases of the bigger shift patterns.

When you are forced to sail close to obstructions the only wind you get is that which comes over the obstruction or, in the case of trees and undergrowth, through the gaps. In the latter case the combination of wind that comes over and wind that comes through leads to a lowest wind speed at a distance from the trees of about five times their height. You can gauge this distance by using a hand yardstick as shown in Fig. 5.3. You will get more wind close in by trees with open gaps between them,

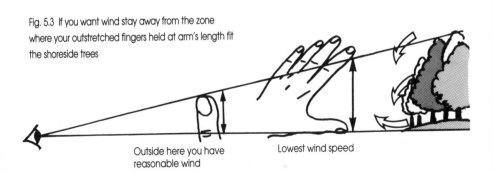

Fig. 5.3 If you want wind stay away from the zone where your outstretched fingers held at arm's length fit the shoreside trees

Outside here you have reasonable wind

Lowest wind speed

and of course the wind will pick up something like its unobstructed speed much further out.

Overriding all obstructions will come the gusts. These come down as if on an escalator over the obstructions and so you will get, in the shadow of cliffs, on rivers, etc., places where there is almost no wind apart from the sudden appearance of the gusts, which then seem much stronger as they collide with air that is almost still. This situation can be very difficult for both dinghies and boards, especially the latter.

6 COASTS AND WIND

The direction in which a coast faces makes considerable difference to the wind regime it experiences. It is usual for a coastal place to experience more on-shore breezes than off-shore ones during the spring and summer. Daytime winds tend to be stronger than nighttime ones and so during these seasons more air comes ashore by day than returns to it by night. In autumn and winter the reverse may be true.

The on-shore seabreezes are powered by the sun shining on the coastal landmass and especially on hill slopes facing the sun, and so an east-facing coast will start up the seabreeze powerhouse earlier than a south-facing one. West-facing coasts may have to wait until afternoon before the full seabreeze driving power is attained, while north-facing coasts which are not flat may have a very weak seabreeze regime altogether.

We cannot forget also that the prevailing winds are generally westerly and so east coasts are sheltered from many of the normal winds that blow, while south coasts and north coasts are more or less neutral to them and west coasts bear the full brunt.

We are considering here the general run of a long coastline, but we know that few coastlines are straight. Bays are bitten out and headlands project from them, while the convoluted waterways of creeks and harbours may point in any direction. So when we speak of a coast with a certain orientation, such as east, we only mean that on the whole the coast stretches in a north–south line.

Estuary sailing means sailing up the rivers and creeks that extend inland from the main sea coast in question. They must have a majority of their lengths lying perpendicular to the coast and so will provide side-shore winds when the major wind blows on-shore or off-shore. *Enclosed waters* mean coastal lagoons, étangs, lakes or reservoirs and these will experience conditions much like the main sea coast so long as they lie within about ten miles (16 km) of it.

Long-term windshifts

By long-term we mean shifts that may take several hours to complete, and once they have happened the wind will tend to remain in the new direction for some time before it shifts again. These kinds of shift are produced by changes in the pressure pattern and are due to lows and highs moving about. The major effects of such wind shifts is to turn exposed coasts into sheltered ones and vice versa, or what were on-shore winds become side-shore winds or even off-shore winds.

The basic rule for wind shifts when bad weather systems are approaching is:

- Winds back (shift anticlockwise) ahead of bad weather.

The basic rule for wind shifts when fronts pass is:

- Winds veer (shift clockwise) when fronts pass.

These rules imply that the depression has a centre that will track to the north of you; in Atlantic Europe, south of Scandinavia, this is most often the case.

Changeable weather

The normal sequence of weather when it is described as 'changeable' is governed by relatively short-lived ridges of high presure where weather is good followed by longer periods of disturbed weather when troughs of low pressure pass.

The normal sequence of wind shifts, starting in the good weather ridge, is:

1. Wind mainly W and not above Force 4 – usually less.

2. This wind backs towards south as cloud encroaches overhead and often increases.

3. It remains in the southerly direction (between SE and SW) while rain falls.

4. It then veers as the rain ceases and the warm front passes. The weather gets a distinctly warmer – even muggy – feel to it.

5. The wind stays in the veered direction (maybe SW to W) under mainly cloudy skies.

6. When the cold front strikes the wind again veers (see Photo 3). There are often squalls of wind and rain (or hail) at first.

7. These are followed by rain that lightens and eventually ceases as the cloud of the cold front breaks to clear skies. The wind direction is now typically NW and the air is fresher and given to building heap clouds (cumulus and cumulo nimbus). Showery weather often follows, but does not have to do so.

8. Any showers then die out and fair weather cumulus develops, especially overland. You are now in a ridge of high pressure, which is likely to be followed by a return to (2) above and the sequence repeated as another depression sweeps in.

Fronts and coasts

Winds veer when fronts pass. Tables 6.1 and 6.2 give some useful advice about the likely conditions when the forecasts are for fronts passing through an area, using the southwest corner of England and Wales as an example (see Fig.6.1 on page 46). In the case of occluded fronts read warm front and cold front, leaving out asterisked sections and toning down the cold front weather.

TABLE 6.1 WARM FRONT EXPECTED

Front	Wind direction	Weather	Wave conditions	New situation
Before the front passes	Normally around S–SE	Increasing cloud. Overcast skies. Rain.	May grow dangerously high on coasts facing the wind, i.e. almost anywhere on the south coast of England.	Not applicable.
When the front has passed*	Normally SW–W	May be a break as front passes but normally cloudy. Can be rain, drizzle, low cloud or fog.	Previously vulnerable coasts such as A–B, C–D, E and F will now be sheltered so inshore waves decrease even if wind stays up.	Previously sheltered coasts such as P–R and T–U grow bigger waves.

Photo 3 Cold fronts can produce nasty squalls so keep an eye out for them. The great solid mass of clouds – sometimes with anvil tops – says that this is no ordinary shower.

TABLE 6.2 COLD FRONT EXPECTED

Front	Wind direction	Weather	Wave conditions	New situation
Before the front passes	Normally SW–W	Often cloudy but there may be a break just before the front.	Wave conditions should not change appreciably from what they were before.	Not applicable.
As the front passes	Often sharp veer to NW or even N	Big gusts and squalls very often. Sometimes thunder. Confused seas and cloud patterns.	Some coasts will have a dramatic change to lower inshore waves while others will suddenly become rough.	Now the south coasts become sheltered while coasts like R–S and U–V grow waves.
When the front has passed	Usually remains in the NW–N direction	Rain dies out, cloud breaks. Heap clouds with possibly showers developing.	Wind may or may not decrease soon after front has passed but should do with time, so swell should decrease with time and sea as well.	Swell will continue to run in on the Channel coasts of France. Look out for a ridge of high pressure followed by another depression.

Note: You have to listen to the forecast to ascertain whether they expect the front (or fronts) to be strong or weak. If they make no reference allow for it being strong. If weak the winds may shift, but the weather – especially the bad weather along the cold front – will not occur.

Fig. 6.1 Southwest England and South Wales as an example of open and sheltered venues

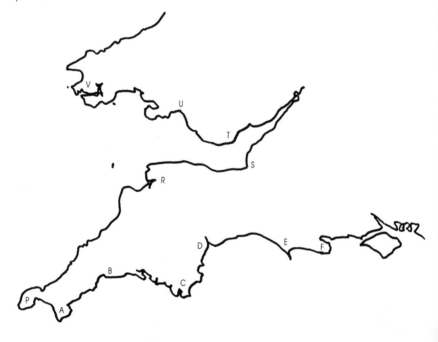

7 LOCAL WINDS

Seabreezes

Of all sailing types the beach sailor is the one most affected by seabreezes. These winds that blow from sea to land by day may alter the local wind on many coasts during the spring and summer in Atlantic Europe. The season is longer in the Mediterranean and even on European coasts some quite sunny days as early as February and as late as October can see the breeze pick up gently from seaward.

The breeze is generated by sun on the land and is aided by convection currents. From a practical point of view the latter occur when puffs of cumulus cloud can be seen around the sky. They will not be there first thing and the best seabreeze days have clear sunny early mornings with a wind not much above light or gentle. Then the cumulus clouds begin to develop and not much later the breeze picks up from the seaward direction. This is the description of a 'good seabreeze day' (see Fig. 7.1).

What the breeze will do to the early morning wind depends on which way it is blowing compared to the main run of the coastline. This is summed up in Tables 7.1 and 7.2.

SEABREEZES IN THE MEDITERRANEAN

The wind tables in Part Two show how prone to strong seabreezes the coasts of the Mediterranean are and how these breezes, once established, will blow on right into the evening, often to be replaced by land breezes during the night. However, apart from the fact that the breezes will be able to stem and reverse stronger off-shore morning winds, the remarks in Tables 7.1 and 7.2 apply to Mediterranean coasts as much as they do to European ones. With already on-shore winds the seabreeze effect can raise the afternoon wind speed to 25–30 Kt with corresponding seas. The fact that it happens under clear skies still does not stop these winds being half a gale.

Fig. 7.1 When the seabreeze opposes and overcomes an off-shore wind there will be two zones of calm or fitful winds

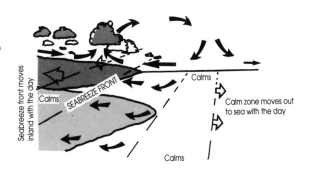

Calms

Seabreeze front moves inland with the day

SEABREEZE FRONT

Calms

Calm zone moves out to sea with the day

Calms

TABLE 7.1 THINGS TO EXPECT ON THE MORNING OF A GOOD SEABREEZE DAY

Wind blows	Speed	Usual sequence of events	Remarks
From some inland direction	Less than 10 Kt at breakfast-time (leaves rustle or vibrate but branches do not move).	The seabreeze force will slow the morning wind and lead to calms and fitful winds just off the beach. Then later will come more purposeful puffs from seaward and soon the breeze will gather strength.	The breeze comes in later if the off-shore wind blows harder. If the latter is in the moderate bracket the breeze may not be able to stem it.
	More than 10 Kt at breakfast-time (branches are moved – tops of trees move fitfully).	The seabreeze force will slow the wind down so that instead of increasing towards maximum wind speed by early afternoon the wind gradually decreases. It will come up later in the day.	Sometimes, on the best days, the breeze may overcome winds of 12–14 Kt but there are often wild swings of direction and the breeze will not last long.
From some side-shore direction	Less than 15 Kt.	The seabreeze force will more or less gradually turn the side-shore wind into an on-shore breeze. The lower the wind speed the earlier and the more positively this happens.	If W winds are side-shore these are more easily converted into seabreezes than are E winds.
From some on-shore direction	Any speed.	The seabreeze force will strengthen the existing wind and it may become quite gusty over the coast. Lower morning wind speeds will encourage the breeze to shift an oblique on-shore wind more directly on-shore during the day, but it may well revert to its morning direction in the late afternoon or early evening.	When the breeze aids the wind, waves can become quite a problem by the afternoon when it comes to launching.

TABLE 7.2 WHEN THE SEABREEZE HAS ALREADY STARTED TO BLOW

Morning wind	Speed	Remarks
From some direction inland	Not usually above 10–15 Kt in Europe.	The seabreeze is a wind without many features. It blows steadily and is a perfect breeze for beginners, although board experts may not find there is enough fire in it. Later in the afternoon expect the breeze to come more from the right, facing the way it was blowing earlier. Early evenings are often calm after seabreeze days and the wind picks up again after sunset. Calm seas in the morning will have built waves by the afternoon.
From some side-shore direction	About 15 Kt at the most.	The breeze may end up somewhere between the morning side-shore direction and the direct on-shore direction, especially if E is a side-shore direction. Speeds may be a little higher than in the off-shore case above, but not much. Evenings do not usually go calm with side-shore winds except when these are easterly. Swell from an existing side-shore wind will produce sizeable waves on many occasions.
From some on-shore direction	May turn 10 Kt at breakfast-time into 20 Kt by afternoon.	These days are usually windy on the beach and may be cool as well. Waves will grow quite large as they will build on the seaway that was there in the morning.

WHEN SEABREEZES WILL NOT BLOW

There can be no seabreeze if the sun cannot heat the land, so overcast and rainy days mean no seabreeze effect. However, it can be cloudy over the coast itself and sunny inland. The breeze will then be drawn in under the overcast. It will not be a strong breeze, but it will shift the wind seaward when it occurs.

When there are showers occurring either inland or on the coast, or both, the showers may temporarily drive away the breeze and the shower clouds will generate their own locally fresh gusts. If the clouds should be thunderstorms, the storms will take over the local winds and drive strong squalls out under their leading edges. Sometimes when the showers cease the breeze comes back.

There are sunny and hot days when seabreezes might be expected to blow strongly. In the event they blow very weakly with sluggish winds not much above 5 Kt. The reason for this odd behaviour is that a 'thermal lid' (an inversion layer) has descended over the coast. Such effects occur only in anticyclones, but they prevent the air that goes inland from rising skywards and so the breeze has no means of escape and we get a kind of breezy log-jam.

Some mornings may be sunny and develop seabreezes, but then it clouds up in the afternoon. The breeze will not stop. It is, after all, millions of tons of air in motion and it will go on blowing for quite a time before it loses its momentum, even when the sun is cut off from the land. Conversely clouds in the morning may be loth to break until after lunchtime. If there is sun and light wind late in the day breezes may develop, but of course they cannot last very long.

FRESH TO STRONG SIDE-SHORE WINDS

When winds that blow side-shore are too strong for a full seabreeze, then a good seabreeze day can have sufficient effect on them to make them blow obliquely on-shore during the middle of the day. This makes the waves bigger and turns some parts of the coast that should have been side-shore into on-shore coasts. However, they soon spring back to their original direction when the sun begins to sink.

GENERAL ADVICE

Some general advice on sailing in seabreezes is given for beginners, improvers and experts at both dinghy and boardsailing in Table 7.3.

TABLE 7.3 SEABREEZES AND SAILORS

Type of sailor	Best time of day	Remarks
Beginners	Morning for starters on boards and in dinghies. Avoid evenings as the wind often develops 'holes' which do not allow board sailors to keep upright against the force of the wind.	We are thinking here of seabreeze days where the breakfast-time wind is from some direction other than on-shore. If it were on-shore and it is a good seabreeze day there may be no time of day suitable for beginniners. Improvers on boards may do well to use a smaller sail, especially as waves are sizeable. Board experts will delight in the sun, the wind and the seaway, especially if the wind has a degree of side-shore about it.
Improvers	Afternoons of seabreeze days give enough wind to make progress; the wind is steady and not full of gusts and shifts. It is a perfect improvers' wind and boardsailors can use a full-sized sail without fear that the wind will suddenly increase.	
Experts	Not usually enough speed for exciting boardsailing except in Mediterranean climes. Good dinghy racing wind.	

Seabreezes inland

The seabreeze current can travel quite a long way inland on good days. As an example, on the South and East Anglian coasts of England the breeze often gets 30 miles (50 km) inland from the main sea coast against winds that are from around NW. In England breezes go further with winds from this direction than any other. These coasts develop the strongest seabreezes in Britain, so elsewhere the breeze may not get as far inland. However, if you sail on inland water that lies within 30 miles of the coast and the breakfast-time wind is light and blowing towards the main sea coast, you can expect a fair day to bring in a breeze. This means that the wind will falter during the middle of the day or later in the afternoon (depending on how far you are inland). A period of frustrating calms may well bedevil afternoon sailing, but usually the breeze picks up cool and clear from the direction of the coast. If you are unlucky enough to be at the maximum extent of its throw the breeze will then stem the wind and a pregnant calm can settle on the water for as much as several hours. At other times the two winds will vie for supremacy, making for wild swings in direction.

Typical times when the breeze may get to inland waters on a good seabreeze day are shown in Fig. 7.2.

Mountain and valley winds

In mountainous areas the most likely kinds of lakes or reservoirs on which sailing takes place are finger-shaped as they occupy deep valleys between the mountains. In quiet sunny weather such lakes will have special winds that blow towards the mountains that are most in the sun from midday to late afternoon. These are *valley winds* which will start earliest and be strongest at the leeward end of the lake. During the night and the early forenoon period, winds blow in the opposite direction, i.e. from the mountains, and so are called *mountain winds* (see Fig. 7.3).

As well as these relatively large-scale winds there are local lake winds which obey the rules shown in box on page 52.

ANABATIC AND KATABATIC WINDS
Anabatic winds blow up hill and mountain sides that are in direct sun and therefore may start early (see Fig. 7.4). They draw in air from the water so creating an on-shore lake breeze. *Katabatic winds* blow down hill and mountain sides and can become strong when the mountain tops are still snow-covered. More normally katabatics will be gentle off-shore breezes and it will depend on the lie of the land

SIGNS OF SEABREEZE EFFECTS INLAND

Breakfast-time wind must be blowing within an arc that is 60° either side of the direct line to the main sea coast.

1. Sunshine at first, but cumulus clouds develop to create sunny spells.

2. Light or gentle wind during the morning (often with many shifts in it) that by the rules should increase into the afternoon, but does the opposite. A period of calm or light airs develops.

3. During this calm a darker line of cloud (the seabreeze front) advances slowly over you. When it has passed the breeze will pull in from seaward.

4. If the individual cumulus clouds of the morning merge and spread over much of the sky during the afternoon the seabreeze may not reach you, or the calm, once established, may persist into the evening.

5. Later, look for signs of a cloud-line moving back out towards the coast. This will be when the wind will come back from somewhere inland.

Note: If the weather is 100% sunny and little or no cloud develops during the morning the breeze may not come despite the heat.

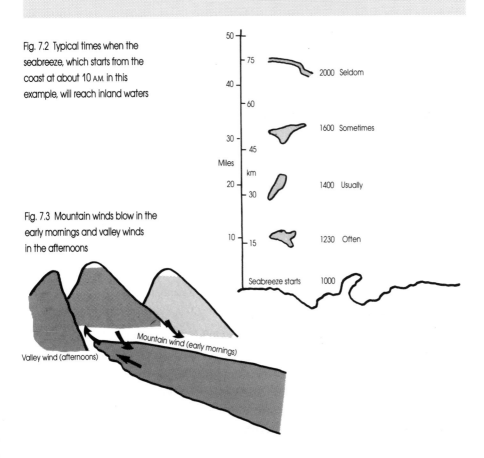

Fig. 7.2 Typical times when the seabreeze, which starts from the coast at about 10 A.M. in this example, will reach inland waters

Fig. 7.3 Mountain winds blow in the early mornings and valley winds in the afternoons

Mountain wind (early mornings)

Valley wind (afternoons)

In the late morning and afternoons:

1. Lake winds blow towards the sides that see the most sun – or the nearest mountains in sunshine (see Fig. 7.4).

2. In the late afternoon and evening (as well as through the night) the lake winds blow from nearest and steepest sides. This means having clear weather overnight.

3. Whenever they can, lake winds will blow along the axis of the lake unless it is not a 'finger' lake, but occupies a plateau area and is almost as broad as it is long.

Fig. 7.4 Lake winds blow towards the sunny side and away from the shadowed side

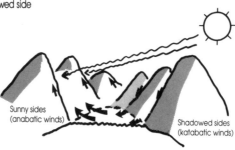

Sunny sides
(anabatic winds)

Shadowed sides
(katabatic winds)

and where you are in relation to shoreside valleys etc. how much or how little of the lake winds you see. Katabatic effects are due to dense air that has cooled by contact with cold slopes sinking onto the water. Thus when a mountainside that has seen the morning sun becomes shadowed in the afternoon, the katabatic process begins to set in. This way an off-shore lake wind can replace an on-shore one during the middle of the afternoon, but of course there must be some period of stalemate between them.

DOWNSLOPE AND FALLING WINDS

Much stronger mountain winds occur when the major airstreams come from the main direction of the local pattern of hills and valleys. Then katabatics are reinforced by the major airstream and enhanced in speed by the constrictions of the valleys (including any waterways) so that locally fresh, strong or even gale force winds can be created, even though the weather forecast does not mention anything like these speeds. These are *downslope winds* and can often be cold as well as squally. The possibility of them should always be taken into account.

Falling winds come from the effect of cloudbursts on the slopes above the waterways (see Fig. 7.5). The rain drags down strong winds that can only escape down the valleys and onto the water and so a relatively calm afternoon is transformed into a ferocious monster that flattens small craft and is all the more dangerous because it was not expected. It is possible that you may not hear the thunder from storms that are occurring higher up but some miles away. The wind will take time to cover the intervening distance but it will be all the more devastating when it does arrive. The advice is to keep an eye on the higher ground for signs of big shower clouds or thunderstorms which you may not experience yourself. That means looking for the tell-tale anvil heads that tower over the lower clouds that may be in the sky (see Photo 3).

Thunderstorms

One of the dangers to small craft from thunderstorms is being struck by lightning. It happens now and again, but it is a relatively rare event. The real danger is from the tremendous gusts that a storm generates and which spread out round their leading edges. The secondary danger comes from the sudden drop in temperature that a storm brings. Before a storm the temperature may be 80°F or more, but when the storm strikes the temperature may fall to below 70°F – in the worst cases 60°F (see Photo 4).

As is pointed out on page 59 the combination of strong gusty wind, a sudden change from sultry hot to clammy cold and the menacing look of the storm as it over-tops you can turn a happy sail into a nightmare. It can be positively dangerous and threaten life and limb if you did not expect a storm and have sailed out in only a swimsuit or shorts with no warmer clothing to hand. Then should the squalls prevent you making it back to your home shore there is a real chance of hypothermia setting in unless you can get some clothes on quickly.

The kind of shores where storms may suddenly produce dangerous situations are those which are backed by high ground that more or less rises out of the sea.

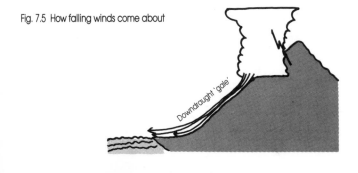

Fig. 7.5 How falling winds come about

Downdraught 'gale'

Photo 4 Not all thunderstorms appear from the land.
Sometimes individual storms form over the sea and if
they invade the beach it is best to get ashore.

Seabreezes can provide the 'fuel' for the storms to feed on in the shape of cool moist air. The lift caused by uphill slopes facing the sea can make the air unstable so that it shoots up to great heights and a storm is created. In its turn the storm creates a great cascade of heavy rain and hail which produces a 'downdraught gale' that sweeps down the hillsides and so onto the shoreside waters (see Fig. 7.5). As it is a falling wind, cliffs or similar features backing the beach will not protect you as they might if the wind were not a cold dense one that pours like water over the edges of the higher land onto the ground and water below.

Even if storms breed further inland, if the hinterland rises steeply they can send downdraught gales sweeping out to sea. You might not even be aware of the storm, but flash-floods can occur down mountain streams that find their way to the sea and the downdraught gales will sweep down the valleys at the same time.

Normally thunderstorms breed over the hot interior of countries, but are most likely where these are not too far from the sea. Thus in Britain the most storm-prone areas are London and Home Counties, while in Germany it is the North German Plain, and in France the area of the Ile de France generates storms that drift up across the Channel and into southern Britain.

THUNDERSTORMS ON INLAND WATERS

When sailing inland on lakes near to, or lying within, mountains, the risk of the sudden unheralded arrival of storms from over the ridges of the high ground becomes considerable (see Photo 6). Because of the downdraughts an otherwise calm lake suddenly becomes a gale-swept maelstrom of capsized craft and whipped-up waters. This is why Continental lakes have warning sirens installed – something not to be found on any lowland water. For example, the Zugersee is a lake just north of Lake Lucerne in Switzerland. Let us quote from *Sailing on Continental Lakes* by James B. Moore:

> The lake is open towards the north and northeast and surrounded by mountains everywhere else. The westerly winds are very fresh, up to Force 6–8, and lash up a considerable sea. Falling squalls occur in the narrows. The Föhn from the south is particularly vicious. In westerly and Föhn storms the surf off the quay wall at Zug is dangerous to boats. Sudden summer thunderstorms have to be reckoned with in July and August.
>
> *Storm warning* Flashing yellow lights operate at Zug and Oberwil. Also yellow flags are hoisted on passenger vessels. The police in co-operation with the Yacht Club Zug stand by for rescue services. In the case of storm warnings it is compulsory for all boats to make for shore at once.

Similar warning systems are installed on many other lakes set in the Alpine Foreland of Switzerland, Southern Germany and Austria and indicate the dangers that can overtake those who sail mountain lakes. It is very easy to drive to some lake shore with a sailboard and get afloat in a remote area. You are by definition the only one sailing and the gentle lake breeze does not appear to constitute a threat. Yet the experiences of the Continental lake sailors make it imperative that you allow for the sudden nasties that can blow up in the shortest of times. Mountains can breed thunderstorms or heavy showers in conditions which might otherwise not favour their growth.

CONDITIONS FOR THUNDERSTORMS

The heat and humidity that precede the outbreak of big thunderstorms are well known. Such storms tend to breed inland because the land becomes overheated and a thermal low forms over it. Such shallow low pressure zones form over land masses while corresponding increases in pressure happen over adjacent seas to compensate. In this way pressure falls over the land and rises over the sea, so that general sea-to-land wind systems are set up which go beyond the normal idea of a local seabreeze. For instance, thermal lows form over Central England on hot days while corresponding highs form over the North Sea and over the Western Approaches to the Channel. Similar effects occur over Sweden's mainland with the attendant high being over the Baltic and the Gulf of Bothnia. A great deal of Continental Europe becomes a great thermal low in a good summer and there is a general flow of wind off most of the Atlantic and Western Mediterranean coastal seas to feed this inland region. Such 'monsoon' air is relatively cool and humid and so can easily be forced into becoming big showers or thunderstorms.

The air over such thermal lows is prone to becoming unstable and shoots up to great heights, forming big cumulonimbus clouds, heavy rain, hail, lightning and thunder. The storms tend to cover a considerable area and to move in the direction of the winds about half way up their height, which means winds at about three to four miles (5–7 km) up (see Fig. 7.6). You can often tell if storms could be routed your way because, before the storms proper, there are tell-tale clouds that look like flocks of sheep or lines of battlements, and the way these pre-thunder clouds move is usually the way the thunderstorms will move if and when they form. Storms do not have to form after these clouds are seen, but they quite often do (see Photo 5).

You cannot rely on the wind you feel before the storms because the worst storms generate their own suction wind that blows towards them and thus is no guide to their movement. The old saying that the storm comes up against the wind is true, but it is a wind of the storm's own making, and the effect only applies to the worst storms. Other lesser storms have winds that blow out of them for quite a distance ahead, or there are storms that occur several miles above our heads and shoot lightning from cloud to cloud more often than they shoot it from cloud to ground. The latter makes a lot of noise and the thunder rolls around the sky, but the lightning is mainly sheet lightning, and so is not dangerous. (This follows because so-called sheet lightning is just the reflection of forked lightning off the clouds as it arcs over between one cloud and another.)

Fig. 7.6 If the storm comes up against the wind, look out for a bad storm with heavy gusts and squalls

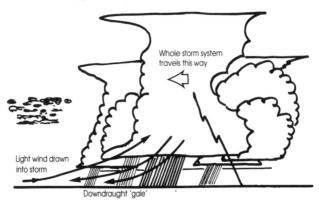

Whole storm system travels this way

Light wind drawn into storm

Downdraught 'gale'

Photo 5 Lines of cloud that look like flocks of woolly sheep or lines of battlements that form on hot, humid days warn of possible thunder to come.

Photo 6 When you sail near mountains or hills keep an eye open for the clouds that can form over the high ground. They can mean danger when they come your way.

The major time for thunderstorms is late afternoon and evening. They may well go on into the night, especially in coastal districts where the displays of lightning may be well worth waching – so long as the storms are not overhead. It is unusual for major storms to breed over the coast itself. What is far more likely is that storm areas that have bred inland will drift over the coast in the evening. However, we cannot rule out storms at any time of day or night and when the signs are there, or the forecast is for thundery weather, keep a weather eye out for signs of their formation. Look for the anvil tops that spread out over the biggest storms and do not be surprised if low clouds obscure the storm clouds behind them (see Photo 3).

Thunder carries for about ten miles, so since most storms tend to move at about 20 mph you have half an hour's audible warning. Lightning may be difficult to see by day, but by night you can judge the storm's distance by counting the seconds between seeing a flash and hearing the thunder, and dividing the answer by five. The result is the distance in miles. (Divide by three for km.)

Visibility is often poor when bad storms are in the offing. The air is heavy and oppressive, and just before the storms break birds tend to stop singing or have very muted songs. Something like the same psychological effects occur with imminent thunder as with Föhn winds. The imbalance in the ionisation of the air, which we experience in normal sunny weather, tends to upset our co-ordination and we become more prone to accidents. When sailing under threatened thundery conditions sail rather more within your capabilities and do not take unnecessary risks.

TAKING SHELTER

Sailing boats may not often get struck, but that does not apply to people on land. Isolated persons and boats drawn out of the water may become targets for lightning strikes. Craft with metal masts and booms can gain some measure of protection by leaving the boom connected to the gooseneck on the mast and draping the boom over the side to where it can contact the sand or shingle. Another way is to roll the boat over and put a heavy weight on the grounded mast top. The weight is necessary to prevent the boat being blown back over by the great gusts that thunderstorms generate.

Boardsailors who are actually sailing may well feel it is best to let the rig drag in the water and sit out the worst of the storm in a relatively safe manner. Boards left on the beach should not present a target for lightning. If they should get struck it is just bad luck – lightning has to strike somewhere.

Sheltering under cliffs or other rising ground behind the beach or around lakes or reservoirs is safe so long as you do not seek an overhang. Strong earth currents run down steep sides from lightning strikes up above; overhangs and small cave-like indentations thwart these currents on their way to earth and so they may jump to you (see Fig. 7.7). However, you are safe where a vertical face meets a horizontal ledge or beach. It may be wet and cold, but choose the open stretches between rocks and not under the overhang of rocks themselves, and if there are isolated trees avoid them at all costs – they are more prone to being struck than anything.

Another possible hazard that is unusual in temperate latitude storms but does sometimes occur is hail that is so large and heavy as to tear sails and bruise, or even concuss, anyone caught out under them. If this kind of large knobbly hail starts to fall you can gain some protection under a sail if afloat or under the rolled-over boat itself if ashore. If you value the skin of the boat more than your own then the latter idea may not appeal, but this hail, when it occurs, can be physically damaging. Boardsailors who are sailing can unstep their masts and drag the sail over themselves as a form of protection.

Waterspouts

These are more prevalent in the Mediterranean than in Atlantic waters, but they have been seen in the English Channel before now. They usually come with thunderstorms but have been known to form in clear Mediterranean skies. It is rare but not unknown for them to come ashore. Normally they are just vertical tubes of spray and so do not constitute a threat other than from their whirling winds. You must lower sail if there appears to be any risk.

Their big sister is the tornado storm spout – a rare but very dangerous phenomenon which occurs when a tornado that has bred over land moves out over the sea. Considerable damage can occur from tornadoes and their spouts, but there is not much advice that can be given. Tornadoes often make a lot of noise as they

Fig. 7.7 If you want to be safe in a storm then brave the rain and hail and do not shelter in overhangs

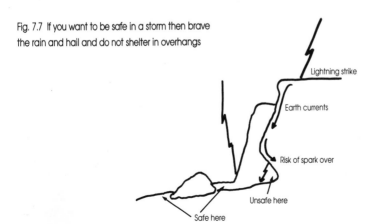

Lightning strike

Earth currents

Risk of spark over

Unsafe here

Safe here

approach and the curiously writhing funnel should be visible for some way, enabling you to take evasive action. Now sheltering beside big rocks, cliffs, etc., does become important. There is, however, a secondary and very real danger that a 'twister' will sand-blast (or shingle-blast) anything within its compass. If you cannot reach shelter then again being under a sail gives some form of protection. This also applies to those mini-tornadoes that form over desert areas and which are called 'dust-devils', as could occur near the shores of North Africa.

Facts about thunderstorms:

1. They need unstable air – big cumulus clouds, massive fronts, heat and humidity plus, sometimes, ascent up hill and mountain slopes.

2. They produce heavy gusts and squalls.

3. The strong wind usually precedes the rain and hail.

4. They lower the temperature to temporarily dangerous levels for unclothed people.

5. The worst ones come up against the wind.

6. The danger of being struck by lightning is higher on the beach than out on the water. There is also more chance on inland waters especially in hilly districts.

7. Sheltering under cliffs and overhangs can be dangerous.

8. Allow for downdraught 'gales' when storms occur inland from you. If you can hear the thunder the storms are within ten miles (6 km). The 'gale' may be with you in a matter of minutes.

8 FOG

Sometimes a forecast will warn of fog risk on a coast that you intend to sail. If there is fog there already you will see it as a long low cloud bank ahead of you. On the beach it will be cold and clammy; sailing is definitely out. There will not be much wind for one thing, but for another if you do set sail you can rapidly lose sight of the shore and other craft and not have the faintest idea which way is back.

On an otherwise fine morning the fog may roll in suddenly from the sea. Again if a low cloud bank blots out the sea horizon make for shore at once. Fog banks can come and go, and so the fact that the fog clears – maybe as suddenly as it appeared – is no guarantee that it will not be back before long.

As fog forms on what may otherwise be beautiful days, seabreezes can bring in fog banks that otherwise would have remained at sea. Thus they are often a phenomenon of the late morning and the afternoon.

Once the sea fog gets inland it 'burns off' over warm land and you should think about an inland sailing venue if one exists within a reasonable distance. On the coast there is no way you can tell how long the fog you now have will last. It might be gone in half an hour or it could linger all day.

Another unfortunate attribute of sea fog is that it likes to form best in the sailing seasons of late spring and early summer. It is much less likely in late summer and autumn.

Land-based fogs are most likely around breakfast-time. They are least likely in the early afternoon, but can come back in the evening. Overcast days do not promote them. It is clear overnight skies that lead to radiation fog that could well be gone by mid-morning in spring and summer, but could linger all day in autumn – as well as some other times of year.

If a friend gets 'lost at sea' due to a sudden clamp of fog, sound car horns or make as much noise as possible to tell them where 'home' is. However, do remember that fog has a nasty habit of misdirecting sound. You may be making a din, but it may not necessarily be heard. However, as the fog moves about, what were no-go channels for sound waves can become conducting paths, so do not give up just because there is no response at first. If they fail to appear within a reasonable time call the coastguard, the inshore lifeboat or the police.

9 ASSESSING THE BEACHES

Coast runs mainly across the wind direction

To reduce an infinite number of possibilities to manageable proportions consider a coast that faces mainly east and includes a small river valley that runs down to the sea, a sizeable estuary, a headland and a land-locked bay. The winds are assumed to come from either NW, W or SW. Figure 9.1 illustrates nine representative beaches, and Table 9.1 describes their different attributes.

TABLE 9.1 ATTRIBUTES OF BEACHES ON AN EAST FACING COAST WITH OFF-SHORE WINDS

	Wind	Waves	Remarks
Beach 1	With SW wind southern end will have some gusty eddies round end of higher ground. With a NW wind there will be funnelling through the gap and increased speed following the contours. With W wind centre reaches are sheltered but ends are exposed.	Only the NW wind is likely to produce any sizeable waves.	NW winds often bring showers and some nasty sudden gusts could occur in the lee of the higher ground.
Beach 2	Here NW wind will leave this beach very sheltered except when showers or big heap clouds appear. SW wind will race along this shore and could be rather more than forecast.	Protected from wave-making effects with all wind directions. Some waves could roll in from offshore when there is wind-against-flood out there.	The little river estuary at X will be inviting but is to be avoided when the wind doubles through the gap as it often will.
Beach 3	Here we have a side-shore beach in W–NW winds but one that needs care when the tide is flowing strongly. The configuration means that the deep channel is close along this shore.	There will be white water off this beach when the tide floods against the wind. When it ebbs strongly the water will be smoother but take care not to be carried too far seaward.	Sailing across river estuaries always demands care so think about it if the wind is directly off-shore, i.e. SW.
Beach 4	Here W wind is truly side-shore but a potentially dangerous shore with shingle banks over which waves will break, so assess it first. With a gentle breeze from SW this can be a beginners beach as there will be few waves, but maybe not when the wind is NW.	Much the same as Beach 3.	A little too close to the deep channel that the tide will have gouged out as it runs out of the estuary, but still OK for local sorties.
Beach 5	A favoured beach on its southern end but avoid the point, off which there will be rocks, wrecks and tide-races. With W–NW winds sudden squalls may come down over higher ground. SW winds will increase past point as will NW ones.	Could begin to build up some waves when the SW wind gathers strength.	This is the beach to avoid if a more sheltered one can be found.
Beach 6	Clear of the effect of the high ground, winds will be fairly true except from SW. A cloudy SW wind that covers Beach 4 can break up to give sunny periods on Beach 6.	Some waves will be generated when NW winds blow.	With a wide mouth this bay probably does not have really strong ebbing or flooding tides so the point is not likely to be dangerous.
Beach 7	The SW wind is likely to whistle along here as the beachlands are so narrow. Otherwise little harm can come to those who sail a beach like this.	Not enough space for waves to amount to anything.	Maybe the best place for evening sailing as the sun sinks early behind the high ground on Beaches 4 and 5. What wind there is left will be found here.
Beach 8	There may not be sailing at all states of tide in the upper reaches of the bay and high water will be later than off the headland. Sheltered side-shore sailing when winds NW and good practice beating back to shore when SW.	No waves with winds in these directions.	Often this kind of shore is shingle with mud flats further out so you need to play the tides.
Beach 9	Less sheltered than Beach 8 but probably a good beginners beach. Avoid the point if you are unsure of yourself.	Waves will only grow on SW winds and then need about Force 5–6 to become worth mentioning.	Same as above.

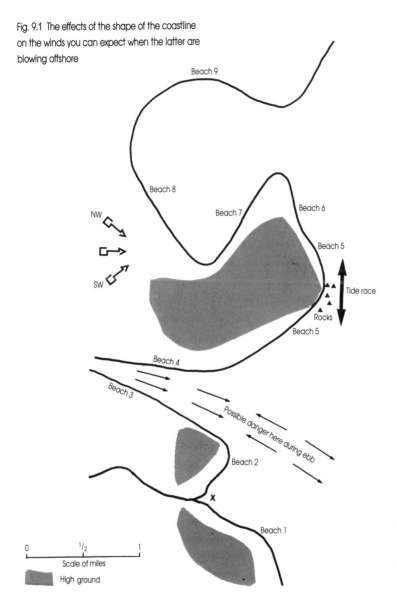

Fig. 9.1 The effects of the shape of the coastline on the winds you can expect when the latter are blowing offshore

Note: The observations in Table 9.1 are generally for days with overcast or at least mainly cloudy skies when the winds are 10 knots or less, or any kind of day when the wind is above 10 knots (moderate breeze and above). This follows because off-shore winds will be opposed by seabreeze forces when the sun shines in the morning, especially when the wind is W or NW. So if breakfast-time is sunny and the wind is light and blowing from land to sea, read the next section.

Off-shore wind replaced by seabreeze

Now consider the same coastline and beaches as illustrated in Fig. 9.1, but with seabreeze instead of off-shore wind. The different attributes of the beaches are given in Table 9.2.

TABLE 9.2 ATTRIBUTES OF BEACHES ON AN EAST FACING COAST WITH SEABREEZE

	Wind and breeze	Evening effects
Beach 1	On calm mornings the high ground sees the direct sun and so an early breeze develops directly on-shore ahead of the seabreeze proper. This blows towards the warmed slopes. Later, when the full seabreeze develops the early breeze will shift to blow directly inland and will increase. The breeze will funnel into the gap at X, maybe starving other parts of the beach of wind.	Breeze will go on blowing around X but could well become calm elsewhere.
Beach 2	Similar remarks to above but in both cases the chance of a breeze developing when the wind is SW is less than with W or NW winds. Around the point facing the estuary the breeze will blow side-shore and could well get up to 15 knots.	The breeze will be thrust back out to sea by the wind it had replaced in the morning but there will often be a period of calm between. Allow for this and do not expect the wind of the day to get you home in the evening.
Beach 3 and Beach 4	With an estuary funnelling in the same direction as the seabreeze expect an increasing breeze as you sail towards the narrows. The breeze will be directed by the waterway and will not often shift direction with the day.	The mass of air travelling into the estuary will be slowed and reversed later than elsewhere.
Beach 5	The breeze will be drawn along the contours and the sea area off the mouth of the estuary will be starved of wind. This shore between Beaches 4 and 5 will have good side-shore winds in the afternoon.	The breeze will be split by the headland and so off the point there may be loss of wind. Another reason for avoiding this place.
Beach 6	This will make good sailing after the morning calms have cleared, but with a full sea fetch waves will grow through the afternoon. Low waves, enough wind and sunshine are to be expected before lunch.	Calm could set in here early, but if the morning wind was SW expect a wind from SW for the evening.
Beach 7	A beginners beach so long as you stay in the confines of the bay. No waves, and wind lighter than on Beach 6. Wind will tend to blow more side-shore the further into the 'bight' between this and Beach 8.	More likely to go calm than coastal beaches but the evening SW wind, when it returns, could be strongest of the day.
Beach 8	Here the breeze will blow on-shore, waves will be small and there will be some reduction in wind speed on the southerly reaches. The middle regions between this and Beach 9 may see most wind.	No help from high ground here for any morning wind direction, so not much can be said.
Beach 9	The breeze could speed up somewhat along this shore. It will become more on-shore during the late afternoon.	Same remarks as for Beach 8.

Note: With off-shore winds that are slightly too strong for the seabreeze to reverse them there can be a slowing of the wind in the afternoon of sunny days. Now beaches backed by high ground may get some odd winds because the sheltering effect of the high ground will allow calms to settle or local seabreeze zephyrs to develop in their lee. Your best chances of wind lie on open coasts.

Fig. 9.2 Similar to Fig. 9.1 but for onshore winds

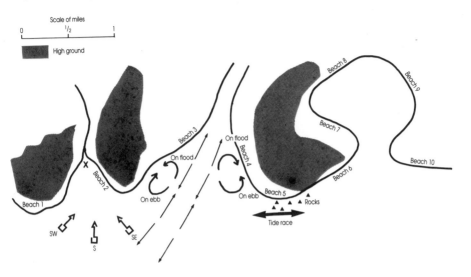

On-shore wind direction

In this example we assume that the coast faces mainly south so that winds from between SW and SE are on-shore. However, the indentations of the coastline make for a whole range of possible venues, as illustrated in Fig. 9.2.

TABLE 9.3 ATTRIBUTES OF A SOUTH FACING COAST WITH ON-SHORE WINDS

	Wind	Waves	Remarks
Beach 1	This is a very exposed location and S–SW winds will speed up along the side backed by the high ground. Winds will funnel into the gap X from all directions and conditions around X could become difficult even if the wind is SW and so X is somewhat sheltered.	Swell waves will run in here with winds from all directions but with S to SE winds there could be considerable surf around X. If river is fast flowing there is a continuous wind against tide problem near X.	A good place for getting what wind there is on otherwise light days. Nevertheless take care; with a SW wind a reach across to Beach 2 might make for a difficult return trip.
Beach 2	Remarks made above about S–SW winds will now apply to S–SE winds. With SE winds this could be a good beach.	Could be some mighty waves on this shore with S–SW winds. SE winds should mean fairly quiet wave conditions here.	The kind of beach which is great in light to moderate conditions but could deteriorate rapidly.
Beach 3	This beach will enhance SW winds, and reaching off across the ebbing tide with the wind against it needs care and experience. Strong SE winds can blow up ahead of depressions and make this an uninviting beach.	When the tide floods the back eddy against SW–S winds can induce big waves inshore.	The inshore end of this beach needs care when the tide is in full ebb.
Beach 4	While sheltered from SE winds the high ground can cause some increase in wind speed here. A very exposed and probably rough beach when the SW wind blows.	Same remarks as above.	When winds are not strong the southern end of this beach may be best. There is plenty of room between shore and the deep tidal channel offshore but keep clear of the point.

Beach 5	Ends of promontories are to be avoided when possible. It is very exposed and rocks and races often abound.	Could be some very white water here especially at lower states of the tide.	Look for overfalls when the tide runs past the headland.
Beach 6	When the wind blows light from SW the high ground will speed it up. If it blows harder there could be some great side-shore sailing here. However, southerlies ahead of coming bad weather could be dangerous.	Waves will always be present here and could get mighty in S–SE winds. Do not go too far off when the full ebb or flood runs.	Probably not too frequented a beach but could be a boardsailor's paradise – if you can get the board there.
Beach 7	Here is the place for the beginner and the improver due to its shelter from most wind directions. With land all round you cannot come to much harm but avoid the entrance to the bay when the tide runs.	Waves will be muted except with SE winds, but swell waves can diffract onto this beach after a big blow.	In cloudy conditions associated with SW winds there can be breaks and sunny intervals here whereas on Beach 4 it will be cool and cloudy. Yet on showery days Beach 4 can be sunny while it pours on Beach 7.
Beach 8	Chance of some funny winds here due to the high ground when winds are SW. Fairly sheltered in S to SE winds and the narrow entrance will take the sting out of stronger winds.	Not much trouble with waves here except for when the strong SE wind blows.	Likely to be a beach frequented by many people.
Beach 9	The low coastline here means that winds as forecast will not be greatly altered by the terrain as occurs on other beaches. Good improvers beach when the S–SE wind blows.	Same as above except for SE read SW.	Another beach that is probably going to be popular and so maybe it would be better to go and find a beach further seaward.
Beach 10	Exposed to all the on-shore winds but maybe out of the tidal zone.	Waves will probably not be bedevilled by tidal flow so better than Beaches 3 and 4.	You will need your wave-launching techniques here but otherwise an improvers beach when the wind is not going to blow too hard. However, think of the morning on-shore wind being added to by seabreeze by the afternoon.

10 TIDES

Under the combined gravitational pull of the moon and the sun, two tidal waves sweep round the earth every day. They are imperceptible on the deep ocean, but when they become constricted by waterways like the English Channel and the North Sea they heap up and create quite large tides which also result in considerable tidal streams. For example, between Jersey and Guernsey the tidal stream may run at nearly 10 knots while where it is constricted to flow past the northwest tip of the Cherbourg peninsula it approaches 8 knots sometimes.

When the sun and the moon on occasions pull in the same direction or in opposite directions, this creates spring tides and neap tides (see Fig. 10.1). When the moon is full or new then spring tides occur. At the moon's first and third quarters there are neap tides which do not rise as high as springs.

BASICS OF TIDES

1. There are two tides a day roughly twelve and a half hours apart.

2. Every month there are two springs and two neaps.

3. At each coastal place the tide will be a spring when it is full moon or new moon and will occur at about the same time of day.

4. The further up a creek or estuary you sail the later the tide compared with the harbour entrance.

Fig. 10.1 How spring and neap tides occur.
The tidal bulge opposite to the gravitational
pull of the sun and moon is due to
centrifugal forces

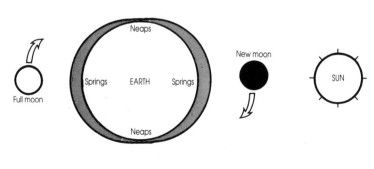

Effects of spring tides

BEACHES

Often there is no beach to sail off at high water. Waves become large and possibly dangerous as there is no shelter from shallows further out. However, you can often sail safely over obstructions that are exposed or just below the water at neaps.

At low water rocks, wrecks and holes become exposed and it is good practice to survey a new beach at low water springs for the possibly hazardous things further out.

HARBOURS

Tidal races in harbour entrances are at their strongest and need to be avoided. Tidal streams in creeks will also flow faster than at neaps, but you may be able to explore the furthest regions of harbour creeks that you otherwise could not get to. However, do not linger or you will literally be up the creek. At low water springs, creeks that have water at neaps are often dry.

ESTUARIES

You can sail up the river on the tide further than at neaps, but beware of tidal bores that can be strongest at springs.

Effects of neap tides

BEACHES

More beach is left to sail from and waves are often lower as they have lost some of their force over the shallows further out. You have to be more careful of possible underwater obstructions off the beach at neaps. There is, however, correspondingly more water at low water and it's not so far to lug the craft.

HARBOURS

Some harbours have potentially dangerous tidal races at neaps as well as springs, but the rates of flow at both ebb and flood are that much lower. Some higher reaches of tidal creeks will be left dry by neap tides, but at low water there will be much more water in the creeks than at springs.

ESTUARIES

There are few problems in estuaries with neap tides, but seek local knowledge about possible hazards whatever tidal regime is in being.

Conditions that affect tide height

Sustained winds that blow along channels and into harbour and estuary entrances push the tide height up and increase the duration of high water. They may prevent the tide flowing out fully and so raise low water. When large-scale winds blow into restricted seas like the North Sea and the English Channel then tidal surges can occur when the force of the wind will prevent the tide falling normally and the next high water will build on the last one.

Sea defences may be breached and craft drawn up above what is the normal tide line are likely to be damaged or swept away. As examples, at Wilhelmshaven on the north coast of Germany easterly or westerly gales can raise the water as much as 10 ft (3 m) above the normal height. Even in the Mediterranean which has no true tides, the water at Genoa rises as much as 13 ft (4 m) when southerly scirroco gales blow from North Africa across the Tyrrhenian Sea.

Tide times

Because the earth rotates once a day under the moon and there is a tidal bulge both on the side facing the moon and the opposite side, so we get two tides a day. The moon, however, moves about 13° round its orbit in a day and this is sufficient to make each tide 25 minutes later than the one before, on average. So if today's tide is high at midday, the next high tide will be about 25 minutes past midnight and the evening's low water will be about a quarter past six.

The time of high water is about the same every day when the moon is full or new. These are given in many diaries, so if you know the time of 'high water full and change' for your stretch of coast you can plan your sailing without tide tables as absolute precision is rarely needed. Figure 10.2 shows how the times of high water increase along the south coast of England from Cornwall to Kent and that the times are earlier on beaches etc. lying beyond headlands that stand in the path of the tidal wave as it moves up the Channel.

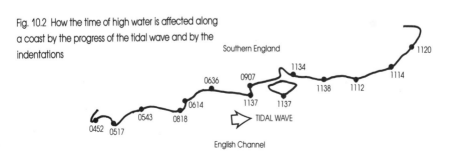

Fig. 10.2 How the time of high water is affected along a coast by the progress of the tidal wave and by the indentations

Southern England

1120

1134

0907

0636

1114

1138   1112

0614   1137   1137

0543   0818

0452 0517

TIDAL WAVE

English Channel

When you get complicated waters like those of the Solent, double high waters can occur in some places, and double low waters in others (see Map 2 on page 152). This means that in Southampton Water, for example, the tide remains high (with a little dip in it) for a considerable period. Then, as the water all has to flow out in a shorter time than normal, it races out. The only way to come to terms with the tides of complex areas of estuary, creek and island in the Solent is to look up a nautical almanac or the pilot for the area. The almanac will also give the exact times of high and low water plus the tidal range, but it is not practical to expect most dinghy and boardsailors to have one. Tide tables are often printed for local yacht chandlers and tide times are displayed at many coastal resorts – often near the pier – or they can be obtained from the harbour master's office or the coastguard (or the equivalent in other countries). Once you know the time of the tide for one day you then know it *roughly* for the next day by adding an hour, but do not extend this too many days ahead or you may get out of phase with the true times of high and low water.

When you sail at the head of a tidal creek you must allow for the tide being later than on the main sea coast. In tidal rivers high water may be an hour or more later depending on how far up the river you happen to be. A creek that runs in five or six miles from the sea may have high water as much as half an hour later than at the harbour entrance.

Finding high water full and change (HWFC)

Once you have tide tables it is fairly easy to find the time at which the tide will be high at full moon and new moon. This time does not vary very much so once you have found it you will simply have to look in a diary, or a newspaper, at the phases of the moon to see whether a tidal place will have any water or not. So even when you have lost your tide tables or just do not have any you can assess the state of the tide.

We can see how to find HWFC from an example. Table 10.1 is based on the tide tables for Harwich in Essex. (They normally print solid circles for the full moon and open circles for the new moon.) The highest tides run about two days behind the moon. According to the table, we find that the average of accurate times is 1307. We shall not be far out, then, if we take it that the tide will be high at 1 P.M. GMT every time the moon is full or on the change (new).

At the heads of creeks you can usually get out two hours either side of high water, but only experience will reveal all the tidal quirks of small waters.

The tide tables also tell you the difference of high water on the Standard Port (in the example above, Harwich). Suppose you want to sail from the tidal estuary of the

TABLE 10.1 ESTIMATING TIME OF HIGH WATER FULL AND CHANGE

New Moon	Full Moon	Add two days	Time of high water (GMT)
	Jan 7	Jan 9	1253
Jan 21		Jan 23	1256
	Feb 6	Feb 8	1324
Feb 20		Feb 22	1306
	Mar 7	Mar 9	1304
Mar 22		Mar 24	1304
	Apr 6	Apr 8	1323
Apr 21		Apr 23	1302

River Colne at the old fishing village of Wivenhoe. The tables tell you that you have to add 25 minutes to Harwich's times so, again, as exact accuracy is not important, you can remember that HWFC for Wivenhoe is about 1.30 P.M. As your diary tells you it is a new moon today you know that it will not be worth getting to the water before about 12.30 and that you will have to be back by about 4.30 or face a tramp through the mud.

Tidal range

The amount that the tide rises and falls at any place is called the *tidal range*, and Fig. 10.3 shows what is meant by the terms used in nautical almanacs. The average values of the height of the tide above a fixed level – called the 'chart datum' – are referred to as mean values and so we get:

MHWS = mean high water springs
MLWS = mean low water springs

The difference between these two heights is called the 'spring range'. Similarly we have:

MHWN = mean high water neaps
MLWN = mean low water neaps

and the difference between these two is called the 'neap range'. The spring range is always considerably larger than the neap range, except in some special places which we will refer to.

The range of the tide depends on where you sail. On the English south coast the ranges are large both in Cornwall and Kent, so that at springs the tide may rise and fall over 20 ft (6 m) between high and low water at Dover. In between these two extremes at Christchurch to the west of the Isle of Wight, the range is very small, amounting to only a few feet. Such places are called 'tidal nodes', and there is a true

Fig. 10.3 The tidal range. Chart datum is a fixed level below the lowest spring tide

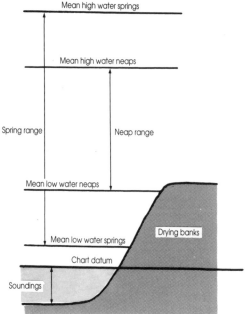

Mean high water springs

Mean high water neaps

Spring range   Neap range

Mean low water neaps

Mean low water springs

Drying banks

Chart datum

Soundings

one in the middle of the North Sea where there is literally no rise or fall of the tide and yet tides rise and fall at all the places on the coasts that surround it.

Wherever the tide has to run into a narrowing waterway the tidal range increases. The Bristol Channel is a good example. At Avonmouth – the port for Bristol – the tide may rise and fall by as much as 40 ft (12 m) and similar great rises and falls are experienced on the north coast of France, especially around the Channel Islands. Such places are not good sailing venues as tidal races abound and you can be left high and dry by the tide in next to no time – often a long way out from the beach.

Tidal bores

We cannot leave tides without mentioning the dangers of bores. A bore is a tidal wave that rushes up the mouth of a river when it has no other means of escape. The Severn Bore at the head of the Bristol Channel may form a wall of water up to 5 ft (1½ m) high and gather to a speed of approaching 14 knots. Many rivers have a tidal bore. Before you sail near the mouth of a river it is best to check whether a bore exists and, if it does, what chances there are of you encountering it.

Tidal streams

The general rule for tidal streams is that they will flood for about six hours one way past the beach you are sailing, and then ebb back for about another six hours. Having said that, the actual details are usually more complex. Again if you really need to know consult a nautical almanac.

What the stream is doing off the coast may not be what it is doing inshore. In general the tide starts to ebb inshore before it does so in deeper water. So the tide will turn and flow the opposite way along a beach before you might otherwise expect it to. Also you have to allow for back eddies forming in the lee of headlands as the tidal stream flows past (see Fig. 10.4). These produce inshore streams moving in direct opposition to the main tidal stream offshore. If sailing near the tip of a headland allow for such back eddies sweeping you out into the main stream before you have noticed what is happening.

In creeks etc. the tide will turn on the inside of a bend before it turns on the outside, and of course, as already pointed out, the time it turns will be later than the published time of high water which will normally be for the harbour entrance.

Tide races and overfalls

Headlands are very bad places to sail from. There are more possible hazards off headlands than anywhere, and two of these hazards are tidal races and overfalls. A tidal race develops past a headland because the flood or the ebb becomes squeezed and constricted (Fig. 10.4) so it races past the headland. At the same time lines of rocks may well jut out across the race. They are the remains of the headland before weather and tides caused it to crumble into the sea. The stream tumbles and falls

Fig. 10.4 How tide races and back eddies form around headlands

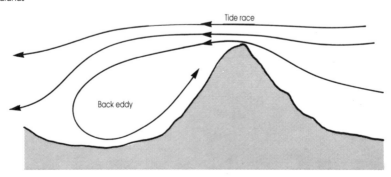

over these rocks and creates hazardous conditions for any craft that gets caught in them. They are especially dangerous when the wind blows at all strongly. If there is even a moderate wind blowing against a tidal race then the waves seethe and break and you imagine you are in a maelstrom.

The most likely places for the production of races, eddies and overfalls are where there is a scattering of islands. Accordingly ones are found in the Channel Islands and around the Western Isles of Scotland. To quote one example from *Reed's Nautical Almanac*: 'Race of Alderney: maximum spring rate 7–9½ knots, neap rate 5½ knots. With wind and tide in opposition – seas break heavily. Heavy overfalls over submerged rocks and banks.' Not a good place to be!

The twelfths rule

You can estimate how high the tide has risen above low water or fallen below high water using the twelfths rule:

1. Divide the range of the tide by twelve.

2. In the first hour after low water the tide rises one twelfth. In the second hour it rises a further two twelfths making three in all, i.e. the tide is a quarter of the way up.

3. In the third and fourth hours it rises three twelfths and so is three quarters up.

4. In the fifth hour it rises two twelfths and finally a twelfth in the sixth hour.

All these times and heights are approximate, and so the fact that in creeks we have a regime of seven hours going out and five hours coming in is not a drawback. You can still make a reasonable estimate of when there may be enough water to sail when you are just contemplating mud flats at low water.

This is all summed up in Fig. 10.5 where the relative lengths of arrows show the strengths of the tidal streams on the flood and ebb respectively.

Fig. 10.5 The rule of twelfths

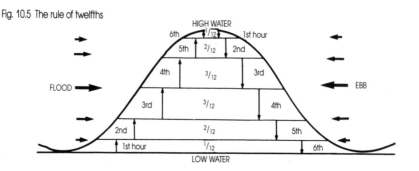

11 WAVES

When you are learning to sail a dinghy and are therefore not sailing in fresh to strong winds, waves are not really a problem except when launching (see page 25). When you are more experienced and race dinghies you learn to use waves to your advantage although they can often be a disadvantage depending on the way you have to sail compared with the way the waves move.

When you learn to sail a board waves are a great disadvantage as the slightest wave will tend to tip you off the board. It is always best to learn to sail boards on sheltered or inland waters, especially if you have not sailed anything else before. Later, after you have been through the improver stage you may want to seek waves for the exhilaration of it or to attempt some wave jumping.

The waves that exist off a coast at any time are due to two wave-making factors. These are sea waves and swell waves:

Sea waves are due to the wind that is blowing at the time and in the place you are sailing.

Swell waves are waves running into your area from outside. They are due to strong winds blowing in roughly your direction, but not actually where you are.

Thus swell can occur with any local wind speed, but sea is created by the wind you are experiencing. The sea waves tend to travel at three-quarters of the speed of the wind and can come from many directions. In this way sea waves can run across swell leading to a rather confused seaway. (The term *seaway* will be used here to indicate the actual waves being experienced which will be the addition of sea and swell.)

When sea and swell run in roughly the same or in opposite directions, now and again a sea crest and a swell crest will coincide leading to a larger than normal wave crest. Figure 11.1 shows how this comes about. Swell is often longer and lower than sea so if we add the sea waves and the swell depicted in (a) we get the seaway (b) that results. Bigger crests and deeper troughs come along, but they come along less often than the crests and troughs of the sea that is running.

It is often said that every seventh wave is a big one, but this is a generalisation that cannot really be substantiated. Suffice it to say that it gives the right idea. When the swell gathers up into breakers as it runs into the shore there is usually a bigger than normal breaker every so many. It is shelving beaches that create breakers and the seaway will normally be much lower over the deeper water. The way breakers are produced is shown in Fig. 11.2.

Fig. 11.1 How sea and swell combine to produce a different seaway

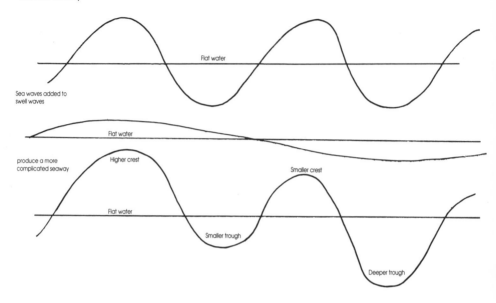

Flat water

Sea waves added to swell waves

Flat water

produce a more complicated seaway

Higher crest

Smaller crest

Flat water

Smaller trough

Deeper trough

Fig. 11.2 How the rotations of the water molecules in waves lead to breaking waves on the seashore

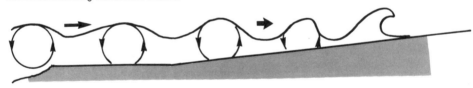

It has been found that the water molecules actually rotate as shown to produce parts of the waves that are rising and others that are falling. When these rotations are interfered with by the shelving bottom the lower parts of the wave-making processes get held back so that the wave slows down. However, the same mass of water is still moving towards the beach and so the wave has to gain height. It is thus exchanging potential energy of height for kinetic energy of movement. The more shallow the water the wave runs into, the higher it has to become, and as the lower parts are being retarded the tops fall over themselves and break. The water thus thrown onto the beach has to flow out below the incoming waves and constitutes an *undertow*. Normally this gives no cause for concern, but when the waves become very large, it can be a potential source of danger. The undertow can sweep your feet from under you and carry you under the incoming waves.

Sand bars etc. just offshore can be the means of taking the fury out of a big seaway and so create lagoon conditions between the bar and the shore proper. However, in tidal waters when the tide is on the flood you cannot rely on this protection, and as the tide rises so the big breakers come into the shore. Very big breaking waves will exist over the bar and if there is a fair swell, even without much wind, a bar can be a dangerous place both on the flood and on the ebb.

The effect on the waves of the wind blowing for a time can be seen on days when there is a seabreeze. At first it is all but calm, but by the middle of the afternoon there are some quite hefty waves breaking on the shore even though the wind may not have blown above about 10 knots since the seabreeze started. This local seaway will then die down to nothing in the evening when the seabreeze dies.

The time for which the wind blows is one of the factors that affect wave height. Another is fetch. *Fetch* is the distance across the water to the nearest land to windward. Wind off the deep ocean has near enough infinite fetch and waves will be at their highest for the wind speed. Cut the distance to twenty miles and waves will not grow to their full height unless the wind should blow either very lightly or very, very strongly. In neither case will it matter to the shoreside sailor.

Wave effects near to a shore

REFRACTION
This turns swell waves that are moving at an angle to a gently shelving shore, so that they run in far more parallel to the shoreline. This is why the waves always seem to run in to the beach no matter which way the wind blows (see Fig. 11.3).

DIFFRACTION
This is the bending of the lines of waves when they run past solid objects like rocky headlands, harbour walls, etc. The technical term for the lines formed across the wind by the waves is *wave fronts*. When wave fronts attempt to pass a harbour wall (see Fig. 11.4) they bend round into what otherwise would be the part of the harbour sheltered by the wall. Solid jetties can produce the diffraction effect and may, together with refraction, produce a confused seaway inshore.

REFLECTION
In some places it is habitual for the high tide to reach the sea walls. When this happens the incoming waves are reflected back out again as they strike the wall. The reflected wave fronts can interfere with the incoming wave fronts and again create a confused seaway with some places experiencing sudden spouts of waves

Fig. 11.3 How waves refract into the shore due to the shelving bottom

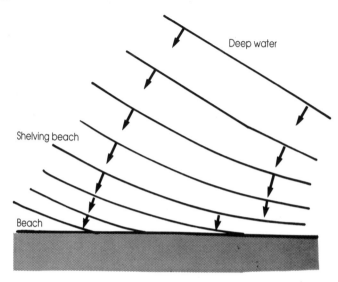

Deep water

Shelving beach

Beach

Fig. 11.4 How waves diffract into harbours round jetties

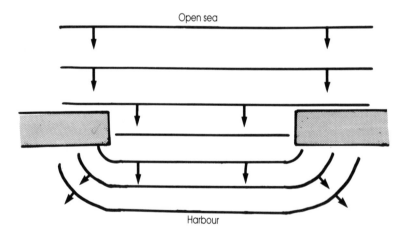

Open sea

Harbour

while in others it is relatively calm. The phenomenon where two sets of waves ride through one another to create a different wave pattern is called *interference*. Thus the interaction of sea and swell creates interference effects that result in seaways akin to that depicted in Fig. 11.1.

WAVE CURRENTS

When wave fronts approach a bay or coastal indentation the distribution of the wave fronts as they are refracted creates a wave current that runs along the beach from the headlands towards the middle of the bay. Similarly a wave current flows along a beach when the wave fronts flow into it at an angle. The wave current travels in the same direction as the waves.

As groynes and breakwaters are put in to prevent the transport of sand and shingle along beaches by these wave effects so you can gauge how prone a beach is to the effects by the difference in height of the sands and shingles on opposite sides of the groynes.

RIP CURRENTS

An immense amount of water is transported towards a shore by the wind and waves and this leads to the water level being higher along a shore with an on-shore wind than further out. To relieve this difference currents, called rip currents, flow out to sea and can be quite strong in places. They need a restriction like a long breakwater, or a pier to confine them and then they can dig channels for themselves. When that happens they habitually flow out along these channels creating a current that runs the unsuspecting sailor out to sea.

WIND AGAINST TIDE

When the sea is being made to flow against the tidal stream the wave conditions can become quite nasty. The wind does not have to be blowing very strongly against, say, a 3 knot stream for the waves to steepen and break and for the wavelength to shorten to one that is very difficult to manage. Where the stream runs faster than this, as it can between islands and past headlands, one can move from quite normal wave conditions into potentially dangerous breaking waves within a few yards. When sailing near to harbour entrances remember that the ebbing tide is like a river flowing out into the open sea; if the wind blows against it you should not venture near to where the tidal 'river' is flowing. Often you can see the mass of white horses in a strip where the effect is occurring, but at other times, being so close to the sea surface, it may be impossible to see the effect and you will be in the maelstrom before you realise it.

Equally, of course, when the tidal stream flows with the wind a quiet corridor of lesser waves will be created. If it is also flowing in the direction you wish to go it can be a good idea to seek the 'wind-with-tide' corridor.

FACTS ABOUT WAVES

1. Waves in deep water will be smaller than those inshore.

2. The wind does not have to be blowing hard for swell waves to produce heavy shore surf.

3. Wave patterns change when winds shift, so allow for such shifts.

4. 'Lagoon' conditions of small waves on the flood tide can disappear towards high water.

5. Waves can roll right in to sea walls at high water and make launching impossible.

6. Wave conditions can go from acceptable to impossible when the tide turns from wind-with-tide to wind-against-tide.

Estimating wave heights

If you care to study waves from some vantage point where you can see a fair expanse of water, you will find that there is a whole spectrum of different wave heights. Some waves are quite small and not too well formed while others grow solid and able-bodied. The international code for wave height which refers to the larger well-formed waves in any wave field is given in Table 11.1.

TABLE 11.1 INTERNATIONAL CODE FOR WAVE HEIGHT

Code figure	Descriptive terms	Wave height Feet	Metres	French terms
0	Calm (glassy)	0	0	Calme
1	Calm (rippled)	0–4 in	0–0.1	Calme (ridée)
2	Smooth (wavelets)	0–20 in	0.1–0.5	Belle
3	Slight (S)	20 in–4 ft	0.5–1.25	Peu agitée
4	Moderate (M)	4–8	1.25–2.5	Agitée
5	Rough (R)	8–13	2.5–4	Forte
6	Very rough (VR)	13–20	4–6	Très forte
7	High (H)	20–30	6–9	Grosse
8	Very high (VH)	30–45	9–14	Très grosse
9	Phenomenal	Over 45	Over 14	Enorme

The waves experienced off a beach will correspond to the descriptions given in Table 11.1 only when you are far enough out for the bottom not to interfere with the waves and so steepen them.

The height will depend on:

Wind speed

Fetch – distance upwind from nearest land.

Time for which the wind has blown at this strength

and in this direction.

You can estimate the likely height of waves from Table 11.2.

TABLE 11.2 ESTIMATING THE LIKELY HEIGHT OF WAVES

Wind speed (Beaufort)	Description	Remarks
Fetch: 10 miles (16 km)		
Force 4	S	It takes about a couple of hours for the waves to achieve these heights, assuming it was calm
5	S	at the start.
6	S	
7	M	
8	M	
Fetch: 30 miles (50 km)		
Force 4	S	The high seas reach maximum height in about three hours whereas the lighter winds need
5	M	another couple of hours.
6	M/R	
7	R	
8	VR	
Fetch: 60 miles (100 km)		
Force 4	S	It takes a long time (about eight hours) for the seas to reach their full height when it blows
5	M	Force 4–5, and about five hours when it blows towards gale force.
6	R	
7	VR	
8	H	
Fetch: 100 miles (160 km)		
Force 4	S	The highest seas come with the greatest fetch but take a long time – as much as ten hours – to
5	M	reach maximum height. It is therefore rare for the sea to reach maximum height in coastal
6	R	waters.
7	VR	
8	H	

As it is unusual for the wind to blow in one direction and at a constant speed (even within the Beaufort brackets) most wave fields do not reach maximum height. When fronts, or some other cause, shift the wind direction fairly rapidly, this tends to beat down the sea rather than enhance it. When a cold front passes it may make for a temporarily confused sea. Continuous rain, especially if it is heavy, will beat down the sea and, of course, in these polluted days an oil slick will have the same effect.

Note: As most dinghy and boardsailors will not stray too far from the shore they will always be liable to waves that are higher than the waves in deep water. This must be borne in mind when estimating the shore conditions. Even a sea described as moderate may produce very difficult launching conditions when the wind blows on-shore.

12 WATER TEMPERATURE

How warm or cold it is in the water is one of the major factors affecting sailing. Capsizing is fairly inevitable when you sail a dinghy competitively, and falling off is a natural hazard of boardsailing. Regaining control means using quite a degree of energy as you struggle to right a dinghy, bail out and get sailing again. If it happens several times it begins to sap your energy – and that process is accelerated by cold water. Boardsailors who sail in cold waters must allow for the speed with which they may lose the ability to climb back onto the board and sail to a safe shore. The wetsuit obviously helps, allowing a degree of immersion that otherwise would lead to a degree of hypothermia, and in winter a drysuit is important to keep out the cold.

Even so, it is best to have some idea of the length of time you can remain in water of a certain temperature without getting to the point of suffering from hypothermia. A rough guide is given in Table 12.1.

TABLE 12.1 SUGGESTED MAXIMUM TIMES FOR IMMERSION IN WATER

Water temperature °C	°F	Description	Safe (without protection) for an immersion of:
0–5	32–40	Icy cold (I)	Half an hour or less
5–10	41–50	Cold (C)	Half an hour to one hour
11–15	51–60	Temperate (T)	One to two hours
16–18	61–64	Warm (W)	Two to five hours
Over 18	Over 65	Very warm (V)	No normal limit but accidents and the battering of waves must be taken into account

The wind tables in Part Two also give the deep water temperatures off the coast. Temperatures can be increased for shoreside waters when:

- it is late spring to early autumn;
- there are extensive drying banks or sandy or shingly shores which are well exposed at low tide;
- high water is in the late afternoon or evening when water's edge temperatures may get into the very warm bracket almost anywhere.

Temperatures must be decreased for shoreside waters:

- when it is late autumn through the winter into spring;
- when, again, there are extensive drying banks as detailed above;
- when high water occurs in the early morning through to late morning then water's edge temperatures should be decreased by a bracket.

The water gains heat as it floods over drying banks, beaches, mud flats, etc., which have been irradiated by the sun, and it loses heat when it floods over similar areas that have lost heat overnight by radiation. Thus the biggest variations are in clear weather when it is sunny by day and starry by night. In winter the water's edge freezes first and then deeper water in creeks etc. The sea proper never freezes in temperate latitudes because of the salt content which makes its freezing temperature lower than the normal freezing point of pure water (0°C or 32°F).

In tideless areas like the Mediterranean the deep water temperatures are also the inshore temperatures except where the beaches shelve slowly. In such cases both temperatures can be experienced. Equally the water temperatures around small islands will not vary as much as they will on mainland areas of creek and estuary.

Inland waters have temperatures that will increase only by the uptake of the sun's heat. Shallow lakes with shelving shores will become warm very quickly in a good spring and retain a lot of the heat into autumn. However, the reservoir that has a constant throughput of water will often remain cold as the incoming water also will usually be cold and will not have time to warm up effectively before being drawn off for use.

Finger and other deep water lakes will remain cold throughout the year and should be treated with respect, as they can also have very sudden clamps of weather and wind.

Inshore water temperatures

TIDAL LARGE-WATER BEACHES
The shore-side waters that lie between high and low water will tend to follow Table 12.2 below for estuary waters, but only when there are extensive areas of sand etc. will they get as warm by day or as cold by morning as indicated. In general shoreside waters are warmer than deep sea temperatures (as given in Part Two) in late spring and summer and colder in late autumn and winter.

NON-TIDAL LARGE-WATER BEACHES
Here it depends on the depth of water off the beach how much warmer or cooler the shoreside waters are. The only way the water can acquire heat is by direct absorption of radiation so the water needs to be shallow. If it becomes deep close offshore the inshore waters will be the same temperature as the deep waters and only along the edges will the temperature be much higher. Equally only by losing radiation by night can the shoreside waters cool down. This is an inefficient process and so Mediterranean summer water temperatures become very warm indeed.

NON-TIDAL ESTUARY BEACHES

May be cold or even very cold when streams from high ground inland are in spate. Also these may suffer from flash floods when heavy rains occur inland. These may not occur on the coast or even, sometimes, be evident from the coast. Thus forecasts of thunderstorms or heavy rains should make one wary of such rivers and their estuaries.

TIDAL ESTUARY BEACHES

The warmth of the waters in creeks, harbours and estuaries can be assessed from Table 12.2. The descriptions refer to days which are mainly sunny and to nights which are mainly clear. With overcast skies there will be no variations worth mentioning.

TABLE 12.2 WATER TEMPERATURE AT TIDAL ESTUARY BEACHES (SPRING–AUTUMN)

Low water at	Next high water	Next low water	Following high water	Next low water
Midnight	0600 Cold	Midday Cold	1800 Warm	0100 Warm
0300	0900 Cold	1500 Cool	2100 Neutral	0400 Neutral
0600	Midday Neutral	1800 Warm	Midnight Warm	0400 Neutral
0900	1500 Very warm	2100 Warm	0300 Cool	1000 Cold
Midday	1800 Very warm	Midnight Very warm	0600 Neutral	1300 Warm
1500	2100 Warm	0300 Neutral	0900 Cool	1600 Warm

Remember that when sailing off a beach that you have to allow not for the water as it feels on launching, but for the temperature further out, which can be many degrees lower.

Summary of temperatures for Atlantic Europe

Table 12.3 gives a general summary of sea, inland water and air temperatures for Atlantic coasts of Europe. More specific details are given in Part Two.

TABLE 12.3 ATLANTIC EUROPE – TEMPERATURE SUMMARY

Months	Sea temperatures	Inland waters	Air temperatures
January – February	*Inshore* Very cold, maybe near or below 0°C in spells of icy water. *Offshore* At their lowest but not usually below 5°C (41°F) although lower off Denmark and in Baltic. Up to 11° or 12°C on Biscay coasts.	Shallow lakes freeze easily, deeper lakes may not but water very cold. Rivers only freeze in sustained cold weather. Reservoirs freeze easily.	Normally at its lowest but in some Februaries it is warmer than in March or even April.
March – April	*Inshore* Some increase but can still be very cold in creeks and harbours. *Offshore* Not much change in March but rapid increase in April.	No increase in deep lake water and very little in rivers. Reservoirs and shallow lakes see some increase.	Rapid increase in temperature on sunny days but often cold with night frosts and even snow.
May – June	*Inshore* Very rapid increase in tidal waters that feed creeks and harbours. Edge water can be warm on afternoon high waters. *Offshore* Sharp increase in warmth as sun climbs to maximum elevation.	Lake waters gain slowly but always cold except where shores shelve gently. Cold where rivers and streams run into lakes. Reservoirs really warm up but rivers follow more slowly.	Very rapid rise in warmth by day but can still be night frosts in May and even snow.
July – August	*Inshore* Highest shoreside temperatures towards end of this period except where shores shelve steep-to where it can be cold. *Offshore* Temperatures reach maximum at end of August but still lower than inshore. Generally 15–16°C in Channel and North Sea, 18–20° in Biscay and 13–15° off Ireland, Scotland and Norway.	Shallow lakes and reservoirs at maximum temperature. Deep lakes also at maximum but still cold.	Top of the temperatures but sometimes September can be warmer than August.
September – October	*Inshore* Longer nights mean creek temperatures fall but coastal waters still high in September. Accelerating drop in October. *Offshore* Deeper water temperatures remain high in September but start to fall rapidly in October.	Lakes at the highest they are going to be. Reservoirs etc. maintain temperature but become considerably colder late October.	Air temperatures wane slowly, being held up by sea temperatures, but in Continental Europe temperatures fall rapidly into October.
November – December	*Inshore* Long nights cool tidal waters very rapidly as well as coastal waters that wash gently shelving beaches. *Offshore* Deeper waters cool but still retain echoes of summer's warmth.	Lakes cool slowly. Reservoirs cool rapidly. Most rivers will be getting very cold.	Air temperatures are still held higher than might be expected by the storage-heater effect of the sea. In Continental Europe temperatures will have fallen to icy on many occasions.

WATER TEMPERATURE

13 CLOTHING

It is recommended that a neoprene wetsuit is worn for boardsailing at all temperatures below 24°C or 75°F. You might not feel you need one when sailing on a well-frequented reservoir or lake at these temperatures, especially if there is a rescue boat in attendance. However, whenever you go boardsailing out onto the open sea the 'long john' part of the wetsuit is a must if for no other reason than it protects your legs from the damage that the edges of a board can produce.

Under this you will wear a swimsuit and you must wear sneakers or special sailing shoes to protect your feet from underwater hazards like rocks, remains of wrecks, etc. In waters that spawn such things shoes will protect you should you step on a sea-urchin; you will not then end up with festering sores where the poisonous spines have broken off in your skin. In other places shoes prevent cuts from broken glass and the sharp edges of shells, or the grazes you can get from barnacles on groynes.

Dinghy sailors need a wetsuit or a drysuit. In the latter case you wear an insulating layer of ordinary clothes under the suit. These can include thermal underwear and sweaters or the special cellular underwear produced for sailing that is quick-drying. A true drysuit will have waterproof bands at the cuffs and ankles and around the neck which is important for winter sailing in temperate latitudes. The dinghy sailor will expect to get wet when capsizing or when 'shipping water' over the bow, but comfort and ease of movement often mean that a waterproof jacket and shorts are worn plus short socks in sailing shoes. Otherwise waterproof long trousers are added when it gets really nasty. Most of the body heat is lost from the top of the head as well as through hands and feet, so when it is very windy and cold wear a woolly hat and special waterproof gloves.

An absolute must for both dinghy and boardsailors is a buoyancy aid or lifejacket. This latter may be included in a sailing jacket as an inflatable inner liner that has a mouthpiece close to the mouth so that it can be blown up when required. There are also automatically inflatable types but these do not have the inherent buoyancy of the mouth-inflatable types, though they are less restricting. Most boardsailors use a buoyancy aid of fixed buoyancy which should produce a minimum of 16 lb (over 7 kg) of inherent buoyancy.

The sea reflects a great deal of the sun's radiation and so in summer – and especially in Mediterranean or similar locations – you will need sunglasses as well as protection for the top of the head and the nape of the neck. Sunglasses and sailing do not go well together as just at a moment of stress they are likely to drop off and get lost overboard. It is essential to attach a cord (or maybe elastic) squarely to the arms of the glasses and position it round the back of the head. A panama hat may not seem to go well with sailing either, but if it prevents sunstroke then it is worthwhile.

Barrier creams, especially on parts that directly face the sun such as the top of the nose, should be applied where necessary. It is so easy in the cooling wind to forget that the sun still blazes and you can get as sunburnt sailing as lying on the beach.

Table 13.1 gives some recommendations.

TABLE 13.1 RECOMMENDATIONS FOR CLOTHING

Water temperature °C	°F	Description	Remarks
0–5	32–40	Icy cold	A full-water-resistant dry suit, gloves and a hat. Sail well within your capabilities. Have pre-inflated buoyancy in case your hands go numb. Avoid capsizing or falling off a board if you can! Only organised events should be attempted in these temperatures.
5–10	41–50	Cold	A full drysuit or wetsuit is a must plus a hat. Again do not be adventurous unless backed up by a rescue boat.
11–15	51–60	Temperate	Local board sorties with others can be undertaken with the long john part of a wetsuit and windproof top clothing. Windproof jacket and jumper. Shorts can be worn.
16–20	61–68	Warm	*Boards* Long johns and a tee shirt are often enough unless going for extended trips with another or alone. *Dinghies* Shorts and a shirt are often enough.
21–25	69–77	Very warm	*Boards* Go in your swimsuit but take care not to scrape yourself on edge of skegs etc. *Dinghies* Can be sailed in shorts and shirts – or no shirts.
26–30	78–86	Tepid	Not much to say here except take your soap and have a bath.

How will it feel

By definition, if you are going to sail you have to have some wind. Since wind makes any air temperature seem cooler we need to know what the 'wind-chill' factor is. We have to do this on the 'sensation value' of the airstream that blows past us – whether it *feels* warm or cool or cold – but this also depends on acclimatisation. Scandinavians will be accustomed to cooler overall temperatures than those who live around the 50th parallel, while the latter will feel the heat more than the Italians and the Greeks. As we cannot allow for everyone, the 'sensation' values given in the following tables are for those living around the 50th parallel; people living in cooler or warmer climes will have to adjust accordingly.

The other factor is the acclimatisation one undergoes during the year. We get used to winter cold and summer heat and so may find spring and autumn temperatures more trying as they so often switch from one to the other – especially spring temperatures. We have given two tables to allow in some measure for this –

Table 13.2 is for spring and autumn, and Table 13.3 is for summer. The descriptions follow those used by the forecasters, but have been modified a little here and there. Since very little risk is involved with air temperatures over 20°C (about 70°F) these tables start with this temperature.

TABLE 13.2 WIND-CHILL SENSATION VALUES FOR SPRING AND AUTUMN

How it feels without wind	20°C Warm (W)	18° Rather warm (w)	16° Average (A)	13° Cool (c)	10° Chilly (cc)	8° Cold (C)	5° Very cold (CC)	0° Freezing cold (F)
Light breeze 3–6 knots	W/w	w/A	A/c	c/cc	cc/C	C/CC	CC/F	F/I
Gentle breeze 6–10 knots	w	A	c/cc	cc/C	C	CC	CC/F	F/I
Moderate breeze 10–16 knots	w/A	A/c	cc	C	CC	CC	F	I/D
Fresh breeze 16–21 knots	A	c	cc/C	C/CC	CC	CC/F	F/I	I/D
Strong breeze 21–27 knots	A/c	c/cc	C	CC	CC	F	F/I	D
Near gale 27–33 knots	C	cc/C	C/CC	CC	CC/F	F	I	D

TABLE 13.3 WIND-CHILL SENSATION VALUES FOR SUMMER

How it feels without wind	20°C Normal (N)	18° Rather cool (c)	16° Cool (cc)	13° Very cool (C)	10° Cold (CC)
Light breeze 3–6 knots	N/c	c/cc	cc/C	C/CC	CC
Gentle breeze 6–10 knots	c	cc	C	CC	
Moderate breeze 10–16 knots	c/cc	cc/C	C/CC	CC	
Fresh breeze 16–21 knots	cc	C	CC	CC	
Strong breeze 21–27 knots	cc/C	C/CC	CC	CC	
Near gale 27–33 knots	C	CC	CC	CC	

Note: Below − 5°C the air becomes icy cold (I), and at − 10°C dangerously cold (D). Nobody sails for pleasure in such temperatures.

Remember the sensation values in these tables are how it would feel if there were no wind and you were resting. The wind-chill will be higher:

- when in a swimsuit, or if a large part of the body is exposed;
- when wet.

The wind can still chill the body even when the air temperature is above 20°C, so it is important to wear protective clothing when sailing, even in what may appear set-fair conditions. In Mediterranean-type waters and with air temperatures to match, these rules do not apply, but there may be other good reasons for wearing some clothes – certainly a buoyancy aid should always be worn. The only truly dangerous phenomenon that you will encounter on a regular basis is the heavy shower or thunderstorm. The latter can drop temperatures dramatically (see page 54).

14 THE RULES OF THE ROAD

The finest way for the small-craft sailor to become branded a landlubber is not to obey the rules of the road at sea. The windows in sails are there so that you can see what dangers may be lurking behind the sail. One such danger is a ship or ferry that strictly by the rules ought to get out of your way but cannot – or sometimes could, but decides that there is little likelihood of coming to grief in a collision with you.

In general, although the rules state that power should give way to sail, do not push your luck – if it looks as if you are on a collision course with a big craft, alter course to avoid it, and do so early and decisively so that it knows what you are up to. Guiding a ship into or out of a port with narrow waterways is a worrying and potentially hazardous business, and to have dinghies or boards jilling about under your bows can lead to apoplexy. Considering the other users of the sea is the first rule.

The rules of the road at sea are based on what is reasonable. It is not reasonable for a dinghy or a board which can manoeuvre easily to claim right of way over a fishing boat which may have trawls or other nets out and therefore cannot alter course very easily. The same applies obviously to tugs or other boats towing others. The best advice is to keep a good look out and avoid trouble.

There are certain no-go areas off coasts which may be dangerous due to firing ranges or the testing of underwater equipment by the Ministry of Defence etc. If you intend to sail a stretch of coast that is unfamiliar then it is up to you to find out from the coastguard or a harbour master or maybe a sailing club whether any such restricted areas exist.

Racing rules

If you intend to race your craft then you should join a recognised sailing club and will have to learn the racing rules. If you are not racing but come into close proximity with fleets of boats that are, it is useful to know the basic racing rules. It is good manners to keep clear of racing craft, and while they should not be accorded complete immunity from obeying the rule of the road they will think a lot more of you if you veer off rather than force them to tack in needle situations.

The rules are:

1. *Port and starboard tacks* (see Fig. 14.1). A boat on port tack shall give way to one on starboard tack. The definition of a port tack (P) is that the boom is out over the starboard side, and vice versa for starboard tack (S).

Fig. 14.1 (a) When both are close hauled, port tack
boat gives way to starboard
(b) Similarly when running

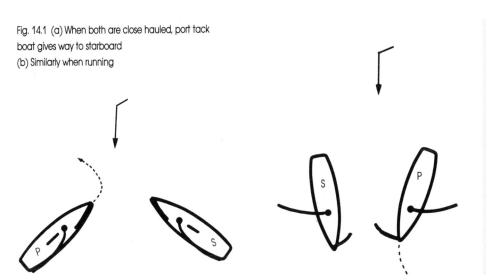

2. *Windward and leeward boats* (see Fig. 14.2). When one boat overlaps another then the windward (W) boat must keep clear of the leeward boat (L). A boat is overlapping another when inside a line drawn at right angles from the aftermost part of the latter.

Fig. 14.2 Windward boat W must give way to
leeward boat L

3. *Luffing* (see Fig. 14.3). Boats on the same tack and in close proximity may engage in luffing matches. Leeward boats (L) may luff, i.e. run up as close to windward as they dare and force windward boats (W) to respond. This implies that the bow of the leeward boat is close abeam of the bows of the windward boat and a leeward boat can luff a windward one at any time until the former has dropped far enough behind for the helmsman of the windward boat to be ahead of the mast of the leeward one. From then on the leeward boat may not luff.

Fig. 14.3 When you can and cannot luff

Can luff   Cannot luff

4. *Hailing for room* (see Fig. 14.4). When a gaggle of dinghies or boards are racing and are approaching something that is going to force one or more to tack then they will hail each other for 'water'. The rule only really applies to boats that are close-hauled and then the windward one or the one that is ahead of the other can call for water and the leeward one must respond and tack. The usual obstructions that have great cries of 'water' rending the air are the shallow sides of channels and large anchored ships, jetties and piers.

5. *Rounding marks* (see Fig. 14.5). Avoid buoys or other marks that are obviously being used as turning marks when you yourself are not racing. The mad scramble for room round a mark does not need the addition of one or more non-racing craft to add to the confusion. You may well feel you have right of way, but it is better to be safe than sorry. If you are caught unawares, especially if fast craft like catamarans and 18 foot dinghies suddenly pounce on you out of the blue, remember that when close to a mark those outside you must give you room so that you are not forced to collide with it. Here you have the right to insist despite their curses and threats.

Fig. 14.4 Hailing for water   Fig. 14.5 Hailing for room at a mark

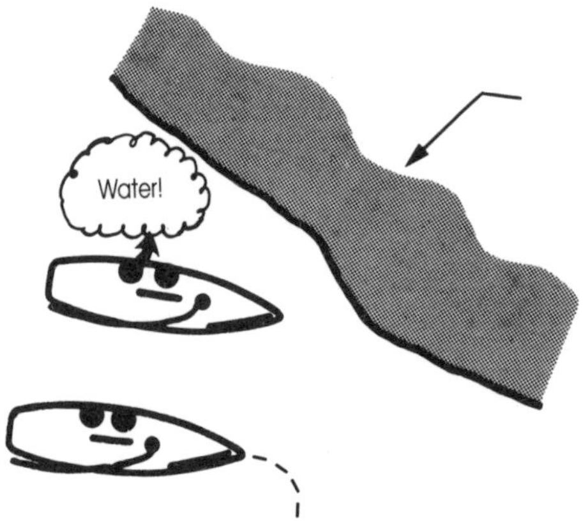

15 BUOYAGE

In busy waterways or anywhere where big ships, coasters, etc., ply their trade in restricted waters, it is as well to keep clear of trouble by avoiding the deep-water channels. These are marked by buoys and the following are the rules (see Fig. 15.1).

Lateral marks

- Red buoys mark the port (left-hand) side of the channel coming in from seaward. These are can shaped. There may also be red spars with or without can-shaped top marks to mark less important channels.
- Green buoys mark the starboard (right-hand) side of the channel coming in from seaward. These are conical in shape. If there are spars they are green and may or may not have triangular top marks.

This international buoyage system of colours, used throughout Europe, India, Australia and South America as well as some Asiatic countries, follows the traditional colours for ships' sidelights, i.e. red on the port side and green on the starboard.

Cardinal marks

There are four combinations of yellow and black pillar buoys which are placed north (N), south (S), east (E) or west (W) of shallows in the middle of waterways. The latter are called 'middle grounds'. Cardinal buoys also mark the correct side to pass a wreck or other obstruction. The differences between the four cardinal marks are shown in Fig. 15.1.

Cardinal marks are not used in North and South America and parts of Asia.

Several other types of buoy exist – for example red spherical buoys indicate safe water, but that is safe water for big ships and not necessarily for dinghies and boards who need to keep out from under their bows. Usually they can sail outside these deep-channel buoys with safety.

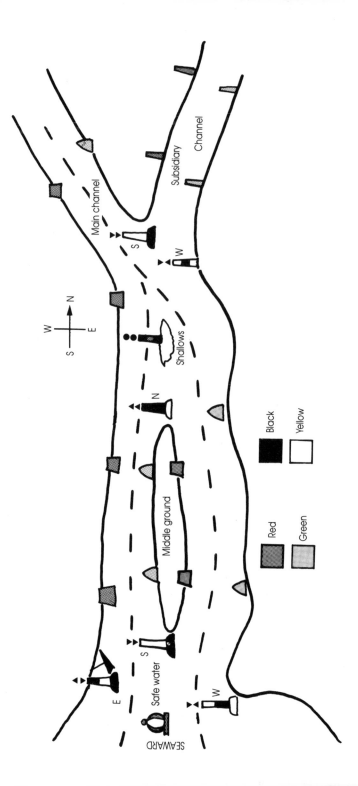

Fig. 15.1 The International Buoyage System illustrated

16 FIRST AID

On the beach or some other shoreline first aid is going to be just what it says – the minimum aid required to get a person moved to a place where they can be properly treated. Table 16.1 outlines a few essential skills that shoreside sailors should master – or at least have knowledge of.

TABLE 16.1 FIRST AID

Condition	Treatment	Remarks
Partial drowning	Mouth-to-mouth resuscitation. Get patient into dry clothes or a blanket. Treat for shock and hypothermia.	See Fig. 16.1 for method of resuscitation. Get working immediately and do not give up – an hour may not be enough. Remove casualty's lifejacket when resuscitation has to be started in the water, i.e. lying in a dinghy or on a sailboard.
Shock	Rest, warmth, fluid (non-alcoholic). Always treat for shock after any serious injury or severe trauma.	Patient looks grey and is cold and clammy. Sweating may be present and also confusion. Fluid means hot sweet beverages like tea or coffee. Rest and warmth as for partial drowning.
Hypothermia	Get out of wet clothing. Wrap in blankets (spare blanket kept in the car?). Rub extremities to restore circulation. Do not try to restore body heat too quickly – no hot baths: a tepid bath will be best. A well-insulated hot water bottle or two stuffed in the blankets is a good idea.	Hypothermia shows when deep body temperature falls by only a few degrees. At first there is intense shivering and difficulty in speaking. As temperature falls shivering decreases but patient lacks coordination and shows confusion. Below 85°F (29°C) muscles fail, pulse and respiration slow down, reasoning ceases. Finally consciousness is lost. Below 78°F (25°C) death ensues. For safe immersion times see page 82.
Sprains	Bind up the swollen joints and give pain-killing tablets (e.g. aspirin). Rest the affected joint. Test gently for dislocation, when some movements will not be possible. If there is movement, albeit painful, assume that joint is not dislocated.	Take the weight off sprained ankles. Support sprained wrists and get proper treatment to ensure that the joint is only sprained and not dislocated.
Dislocations and fractures	Immobilise legs by binding the damaged one to the good one. Splint arms and put in a sling. Swellings or unnatural shape of the limb indicate a real break, and limb must be immobilised until expert help can be applied. Intense pain may be felt where broken bones rub together – possibly split end will come through skin.	Forearm or upper arm fractures can be immobilised by cupping a thickness of magazines round the limb and binding securely. If you cannot make a sling support the arm in a buttoned-up coat. The patient cannot move a dislocated wrist so splint hand and arm together.
Sunburn, heatstroke and sunstroke	Bad *sunburn* can be relieved by rest indoors with copious supplies of fluid (non-alcoholic) until pain and redness has subsided. *Heatstroke* needs same treatment – patient can feel sick and break out in a cold sweat. Occurs when air temperature exceeds body temperature. *Sunstroke* is highly dangerous – maybe fatal. There is sudden unconsciousness and a rapid rise in body temperature. Wrap patient in wet towels and get a doctor at once.	Sunburn is your own fault. Wind by the sea can make a hot day seem cool, but does not alter the sun's power to burn. Acclimatise slowly and use plenty of barrier cream. Heatstroke – or heat exhaustion – sometimes cannot be helped, especially when Northern Europeans go to Mediterranean climates. If the temperature rises into the 90s Fahrenheit (30s Celsius) do little other than rest.

Fig. 16.1 The method of resuscitation

(a) Lay the person flat on their back and kneel alongside them. Extend the head and neck by tilting the head backwards. Clear the mouth of any debris there may be and make sure the tongue is not obstructing the air passage.

(b) Pinch the person's nose and, taking a deep breath, blow into their mouth, ensuring that as little air as possible escapes. Keep an eye on the chest to note when it rises. This indicates that the method is working.

(c) Rest and take another breath while the patient's chest falls. Then repeat the procedure until the patient gasps and begins to breathe of their own accord. Do not give up if there is no obvious response at first.

17 SOURCES OF WEATHER FORECASTS

No one who has any sense ignores the weather forecast. The methods of forecasting today have made weather forecasting in the short term much more reliable and have produced methods for forecasting as far ahead as six days. The computerised production of forecast charts means that very often the general trend in the wind direction is known days in advance so you can do some forward planning. The major European countries are giving five-day forecasts either on selected radio or TV forecasts or on pre-recorded telephone lines. It is impossible in a book such as this to give details of forecast schedules, since these (as well as frequencies) are liable to change. However, this chapter points out the kind of services that are available and where you can get help in finding them.

It is worth remembering that neither land area forecasts nor deep-sea shipping forecasts cover the rather special coastal conditions adequately. The pre-recorded telephone forecasts – such as Marinecall in Britain and a similar facility in France – provide the most reliable source of coastal information. However, if you sail inland then a land area forecast is the one you want, although such forecasts over radio or TV will not cater for sailors. Wind directions may differ widely from the forecast ones due to local terrain, especially when conditions are generally quiet. What follows is a summary of forecast sources.

Land areas

NATIONAL RADIO
Forecasts are given before or after major news bulletins plus gale warnings on selected stations. See newspapers for schedules, or specialist publications such as the *Radio Times* or *TV Times* in Britain.

LOCAL RADIO
This often gives more detailed coverage. Ignore the prattlings of disc-jockeys giving their own interpretations of forecasts; they can be very misleading.

TV
Television gives your only chance to see up-to-the-minute charts, cloud satellite pictures and reliable forecast charts. Watch it carefully – it will all be gone in the blinking of an eye.

TELEPHONE
See the phone book. These can be very reliable for local conditions.

Coastal areas

NATIONAL RADIO
A very sparse service is usually provided. In Britain two such forecasts are given each day and are mainly for fishermen.

LOCAL RADIO
This is much better and is sailing orientated in areas that serve sailing populations. Again find the schedule from the local newspaper or ring and ask the stations themselves. Strong wind warnings are given on some stations, i.e. Force 6 and above.

TV
Again, regional TV services may give some specific coastal wind information, but in general TV will be concerned with the greater number of inland dwellers and their needs.

Deep-sea areas

NATIONAL RADIO
Shipping forecasts are broadcast by all of the nations of Atlantic Europe and the Mediterranean. From French borders northwards forecasts are in both the native tongue and English. France and Spain plus Italy give forecasts only in their own languages, but Greece gives some forecasts in English. Table 17.1 gives the strong wind terms in a variety of languages as may be heard in European weather reports.

TABLE 17.1 STRONG WIND TERMS USED IN EUROPEAN WEATHER REPORTS

Language	Gale or storm warning	Gale	Rough	Fresh	Strong
French	Avertissement de tempête Avis de coup de vent	Coup de vent	Agitée	Fraîche	Fort
German	Stürmwarnung	Stürmischer Wind	Stürmisch	Frisch	Stark
Dutch	Stormwaarschuwing	Storm	Guur	Fris	Sterk, Krachtig
Danish	Stormvarsel	Stormende Kuling	Oprørt	Frisk	Staerk, Kraftig
Spanish	Aviso de temporal	Viento	Bravo or alborotado	Fresco	Fuerte
Italian	Avviso di burrasca	Burrasca	Agitato	Fresco	Forte

All these services give gale warnings, but as Force 8 is too late for the vast majority of small craft sailors they can only advise that the wind is going to rise and so warn you to take precautions with craft in exposed positions when brought out of the water. Figure 17.1 gives the gale warning areas as used by Britain and other European countries.

Sources of information

BRITAIN
Get the Royal Yachting Association's *Weather Forecasts* which contains a seven-language forecast vocabulary (RYA House, Romsey Road, Eastleigh, Hampshire SO5 4YA). Yacht chandlers also sell this booklet which gives an up-to-date and very comprehensive summary of all the forecasts available plus some hints and tips on weather and wind.

FRANCE
There is a folder called *La Meteo* for 'marins, pêcheurs, plaisanciers' obtainable from chandlers, harbour masters and coastguards. It is not so comprehensive as the British publication, but gives useful frequencies, schedules, telephone numbers, etc., plus schedules of radio gale warnings.

GERMANY
A book called *Jachtfunkdienst, Nord und Ostsee* is available from Deutsches Hydrographisches Institut, Bernhard-Nocht-Strasse 78, 2000 Hamburg 4. It gives all the radio, radar and other useful information for boats plying the North Sea and the Baltic.

Note: Do not forget that when you have a forecast of wind speeds of 10 knots or less, look up the sections on seabreezes and other local winds and modify the forecast accordingly.

Fig. 17.1 The gale warning areas as used by Britain and other European countries.
(The N numbers denote the common sea areas as referred to by the nations surrounding the North Sea)

PART TWO
THE WEATHER OF ATLANTIC EUROPE

By Atlantic Europe we mean those coasts between 60°N and 45°N that are washed by or communicate with the Atlantic Ocean. These are also the latitudes that are most visited by the Atlantic depressions and travelling anticyclones.

The weather of these latitudes is changeable. It is less changeable but tending towards bad weather in the northern latitudes, and equally is less changeable but tending towards good weather as one goes south. If changeable means alternating between periods of good and bad weather then the middle latitudes of Atlantic Europe will be most changeable.

However, these are only the most likely turns of events. The summer of 1989 has experienced almost two months of dry and sunny weather. It was the sunniest May for sixty years. For all that time, through May and June, the weather did not change. However, two months of sunny anticyclonic weather is unusual. It is far more likely that short periods of sunny or fair weather will appear between longer periods of cyclonic weather which always threaten rain, much cloud and maybe thunderstorms.

As these depressions and anticyclones chase one another out of the Atlantic so the winds shift direction and change speed constantly. Statistics are only useful as an overall guide. To keep up with the wind trends you must continuously listen to forecasts. For planning several days ahead find out when the five-day forecasts are broadcast or listen to them on the pre-recorded telephone lines.

The semi-permanent high pressure areas such as the one described above for the summer of 1989 are called 'blocking anticyclones' as they block out the depressions from the area dominated by the high. But the depressions then go elsewhere – to the Mediterranean when they are denied access to Europe. Yet even so the chances of having sunny weather in the Mediterranean are much higher than on the coasts of Atlantic Europe because it is so much closer to the permanent high over the Azores. You can gauge this from the figures for the number of sunny days given in the Mediterranean sections that follow. No such figures are given for Atlantic European places because there are so few truly sunny days; the figures therefore give a falsely depressing picture. Cloud may grow after a sunny morning and be followed by a sunny evening, yet that is not what is meant by a sunny day. The latter indicates only a small amount of cloud from morning to night.

You can gain some idea of how Europe fares through the sailing season from the following table.

Month	North of 55°N	55°N–50°N	50°N–45°N
March	Mainly lows	Equal chance of low or high.	Equal chance of low or high.
April	Mainly lows over Scandinavia. More lows than highs over Scotland.	More lows than highs, especially over the Low Countries.	More lows than highs.
May	Many lows in the Western Isles but fewer in Scandinavia.	More lows than highs over England and Wales but equal chances in Low Countries.	More lows than highs, but highs becoming more prevalent.
June	Number of lows over Scotland decreases but more in Scandinavia.	Equal chances of lows and highs over England and Wales. More highs than lows over the Low Countries.	More highs than lows.
July	Increasing numbers of lows in all areas.	More highs than lows over England and Wales and the Low Countries. More lows than highs over Ireland.	Two highs for every low.
August	Lows still prevalent in all areas.	Two highs for every low in North Sea area. More highs than lows over England, Wales and the Low Countries.	Two highs for every low.
September	Number of lows decreases dramatically, but still a more than even chance of lows in all areas.	More highs than lows in all areas.	Two highs for every low.
October	Lows increase in number especially over Western Isles. Number in Scandinavia about the same as last month.	More lows than highs over England, Wales and Ireland but more highs than lows over the North Sea and the Low Countries.	More highs than lows.
November	Rapid increase in number of lows in all areas.	More lows than highs over Ireland and the Low Countries but more highs than lows over England and Wales.	More highs than lows.

Atlantic coast of Spain and Portugal

It is no good applying the above ideas to Spain because they will show low pressure over Spain for the whole of the spring and summer. Yet we know that Spain and Portugal are renowned for their sunshine. This paradox comes about because of the curious way the Iberian peninsula rises out of the sea with its high central plateau. Spain is a cauldron into which the seabreezes blow from all sides, and because all this air has to rise over the higher interior it creates an almost permanent low pressure over Iberia. Yet the air rarely forms cloud over the coasts in summer – and not often inland either; it is too warm for that.

On the Mediterranean coast of Spain the number of days with thunder is between two and four in any month during the three seasons, but the frontier region around Perpignan sees a large number in summer. The numbers will not be any larger on the Atlantic coast than on the Mediterranean coast, even though inland Iberia sometimes has massive storms especially in late spring and early summer. It is the seabreezes that make for storms inland but which keep the coasts relatively clear.

HOW TO READ THE WIND TABLES

HE WIND TABLES

Seasons

For reasons of space only spring (March to May), summer (June to August) and autumn (September to November) are covered. Sailing increasingly goes on in the winter months and those who do so must take the trouble to find out the special conditions to be expected. In general, winter sailors must expect more strong winds than given for spring and autumn, a weakened seabreeze regime in more southerly latitudes and an almost total absence of seabreezes on the coasts of Atlantic Europe. They can expect more and stronger mountain winds and must realise that winter sailing under snow-capped mountain peaks is a very dangerous thing to do.

Time of day

Wind statistics are given for early morning (0700–0900), early afternoon (1300–1500) and evening (1800–2100). These are chosen because early morning is usually before seabreezes blow, but overnight winds are still blowing. Comparing them with the afternoon gives clues as to how strong the seabreeze influences are at any place. Afternoon winds are at their strongest on most sailing days, but this is also the time when seabreeze forces are strongest and can modify or nullify existing winds. Evening winds show how the day's winds are either still blowing or have moved to new directions. We expect coastal mountain winds to have blown away many seabreezes in spring by evening, but maybe not in summer. We expect autumn to show much less seabreeze activity, and wind trends evident earlier in the year to be waning.

Speed brackets

These have been designed with dinghy and boardsailors in mind. Beginners and improvers will want winds in the light to moderate bracket and need to avoid places and times with strong winds. Expert sailboarders are often only happy when the wind is Force 5 to 6. They may not be so happy when the wind grows to Force 7 or more. Thus these are the speed categories used.

CALM
Mainly means that there is more than an even chance that a morning or evening will be calm.

Many means that there is approaching an even chance.

Often means that there are still a fair number of calms, but many more days will have wind than not.

Occ. means that there are occasional calms.

Few means that calms are rare but cannot be ruled out.

FORCE 1–4

Examples will illustrate how to read this bracket:

S means that the most likely direction is south but all others are present.

All (w–sw) means that all directions are equally favoured excepting W to SW from which directions winds are rare.

W–NW (e–s) means that the most likely directions are between W and NW but that winds can come from other directions except the rare directions of E, SE and S. In all these examples the first direction given is the most likely.

NE/SW (e) means that winds come mainly from the two directions of NE and SE but other directions occur other than east.

NW only means that literally all the winds come from this direction. There may occasionally be winds from other directions. Such places are very rare.

W–NW but all means that while W and NW are the most favoured directions the chances of winds from all other directions is not much less.

FORCE 5–6

Here the figures in brackets show the average number of hours with winds of this strength that one can expect at this time of day in a fortnight's stay. Use these figures to compare the windiness of one place with another, but do not be disappointed if you happen to hit a quiet period when you wanted wind or conversely experience a blustery fortnight when you hoped for gentler winds.

NE–S (15) means that winds of this strength come from NE, E, SE and S and that the average season will see some 15 hours in a period of two weeks. Other directions are rare.

All (nw–e) means that winds of this strength can come from all directions, and while some directions may be more favoured than others, do not expect to get many winds from NW, N, NE and E.

NW–SE (n–e) means that all directions between NW and SE through W are included because winds from between N and E are excluded.

FORCE 7+

There are usually fewer directions from which strong to gale force winds come than lighter winds, but the same rules apply here as to Force 5–6 winds.

The — sign indicates that while there may be occasional strong to gale force winds they are a very rare occurrence. If no bracketed figure appears then, while there could be a gale, there is a better than even chance against it.

REMARKS

Where appropriate these have been added to give more detail.

Sea temperatures

The sea temperatures are for the coasts adjacent to the places referred to. In summer right inshore they may be considerably warmer and offshore a little cooler. It must also be remembered that these are average temperatures and in warm years may be a couple of degrees Fahrenheit higher than stated.

Sun/cloud indicators

For Mediterranean coasts sun/cloud indicators are included as follows:

○ Ju–A (17)   This means that the sunniest months are June to August and that on average these months have 17 days per month with very little cloud.

● N–Mr (5)   This means that November to March are the cloudiest months and that on average 5 days per month are mainly cloudy.

N/Mr   This means that November and March are the cloudiest months.

Percentage frequency tables

Tables of percentage frequency of winds from different directions have had to be substituted for the more detailed tables in some cases. This is because the stations involved do not break down their statistics sufficiently. Percentage frequency tables should be read as showing the relative probabilities of wind blowing from these directions at the times indicated.

For example, Porto, on the west-facing coast of Portugal, has, in summer, a fairly even chance of having wind from any direction in the early morning. By afternoon, however, three-quarters of the winds that blow are from the seaward direction of W or NW. In spring, if we lump the on-shore directions together much the same remarks apply to the afternoon winds, but there is a greater chance of early winds from the land than in summer. In autumn the winds off the land predominate in the morning but now northerlies are more prevalent in the afternoons. These remarks indicate the way to read the percentage frequency tables.

WIND TABLES

INCLUDING SEA TEMPERATURES

English South Coast: Cornwall to Isle of Purbeck (see Map 1)

GENERAL FEATURES

Compared to the coasts further east this is a rugged coast with cliffs and promontories, coombes and river valleys stretching down to the sea. Between Falmouth and Start Point the coast is backed by a more or less narrow coastal plain that gives way to the Moors. The Start Point to Exmouth coast turns north and again Dartmoor faces the morning sun. Lyme Bay is backed by the Dorset Downs and is bounded on its eastern side by Portland Bill.

MAJOR WINDS

The seabreezes that blow onto all these coasts will vary locally finding their own way inland through the gaps and valleys. Torbay has its own, often curious, wind patterns and the coast is sheltered from the W, so has a mild climate. Beyond Portland the seabreeze coast of Southern England starts.

NOTES

Allow on this coast for the local vagaries. In particular, if you sail the Torbay coast, ask the locals what happens to the wind, otherwise look inland for the roads from the sea. That is often where the wind will head for or, when from the land, will emerge from.

WINDS AND SEA TEMPERATURES AT PLYMOUTH

	Calm	Force 1-4	Force 5-6	Force 7+	Sea temperatures (°F)	Remarks
SPRING						This coast has more winds in the 7-21 kt bracket than in the light bracket at any time of day or year.
Morn.	Often	E-NE/SW	NW-SW-SE (4)	SW	M 47	
Aft.	Few	SW-E (n-ne)	All (8)	S	A 48	
Eve.	Occ.	NW/SW/E	NW-SW-SE (5)	W-S	M 52	
SUMMER						Plymouth has high ground to the E and NE that brings early morning and evening winds off the land. It shows seabreeze effects both in spring and summer but in other places expect different directions as the breeze feeds round the headlands etc. The strong to gale directions are representative.
Morn.	Often	All (se)	W-SW (2)	—	J 56	
Aft.	Few	SW-S (ne)	NW-S (3)	—	J 61	
Eve.	Occ.	NW-SW (ne)	NW-SW (3)	—	A 61	
AUTUMN						
Morn.	Often	All	W-S (6)	NW-S (1)	S 59	
Aft.	Occ.	All	NW-SW (3)	W-SW/E-SE	O 56	
Eve.	Occ.	All	W-S/E (6)	W-S (1)	N 54	

WINDS AND SEA TEMPERATURES AT POOLE BAY (HURN AIRPORT)

	Calm	Force 1-4	Force 5-6	Force 7+	Sea temperatures (°F)	Remarks
SPRING						Hurn, the airport for Bournemouth, lies four miles inland from the coast of Poole Bay but the land is flat, so while the winds may become stronger on the coast itself, their main directions are the ones shown. This is where the higher land of the West Country gives way to the Solent area, and Hurn represents the lower parts of the coast to the W of it.
Morn.	Often	All	SW/NW (1)	—	M 46	
Aft.	Few	S (nw)	NW-S/E (3)	—	A 50	
Eve.	Few	SW (nw)	NW-S (1)	—	M 52	
SUMMER						
Morn.	Often	W-N (e-se)	SW-S (1)	—	J 56	
Aft.	Few	S-W (ne)	NW-S (2)	—	J 60	
Eve.	Few	SW-S (n-ne)	—	—	A 62	
AUTUMN						
Morn.	Often	W-SW (e-se)	W-S (2)	—	S 61	
Aft.	Occ.	All	SW-SE (3)	—	O 58	
Eve.	Occ.	All	SW/SE (1)	—	N 62	

The Solent and Isle of Wight area
(see Map 2)

GENERAL FEATURES

The Solent is probably the most frequented small-craft sailing area in the world. It is also the most complex with its many inroads for the wind and the complication of the high ground of the Isle of Wight when the wind blows from a southern quadrant. It has many sheltered water-ways and harbours, but presents a problem to the shore-side sailor who has to contend with big ships of all sizes as well as myriad cruising and racing deep-keel yachts. Care must be taken to avoid the major harbour entrances of Portsmouth and Southampton and to obey the rules of the road. Keep an ear open for the hovercraft which ply up and down Southampton Water and across to the Isle of Wight. There are also numerous ferries both in the Western and Central Solent areas. The tidal regime of the Solent is one of the most complicated to be found anywhere and some strong tidal streams exist.

MAJOR WINDS

The SW wind is the most prevalent and most gales come from between S and W, but it is when the lighter winds blow that the complexities of the Solent show up. The Isle of Wight blocks the seabreeze when the latter is fully established from seaward so that Cowes Roads becomes becalmed. The N shores of the Solent are the places for wind. It prefers to blow up the West Solent and, with seabreeze help can be quite strong. With winds from SE or near SE it will funnel up the East Solent and drive up Southampton Water.

The Solent starts the strong seabreeze coast that is cov-ered in the next section, and inland sailors will experience seabreeze fronts on many light spring and summer days.

NOTES

Calshot is the old seaplane base and is right on the water's edge at the entrance to Southampton Water. It is as representative of the Solent as any place could be. On spring mornings we see the effects of the night wind sinking down the waterway from N or NW but by lunchtime the most likely wind is SW, i.e. seabreeze up the West Solent. This story is repeated and enhanced in summer when half the lunchtime winds are either from SW or S, but there are still a very considerable number from SW and W at 0700 before the seabreeze effect can occur. This is the 'monsoon' of the summer months which brings winds predominantly up the Channel to feed the hot hinterland of Europe. This is still in evidence in autumn but then there are more winds off the land at night (and in the morning compared with summer) and a restricted seabreeze effect which will be largely found in September anyway.

Like its complicated tides the Solent has to be studied before its winds can be understood, but those with local knowledge may be prepared to part with it over a pint.

WINDS (% FREQUENCY) AND SEA TEMPERATURES
AT CALSHOT

	N	NE	E	SE	S	SW	W	NW	Calm	Sea temperatures (°F)	
SPRING											
Morn.	20	12	12	6	6	13	13	16	4	M	46
Aft.	11	8	13	14	10	26	6	11	2	A	47
Eve.					[No data]					M	51
SUMMER											
Morn.	15	7	8	4	7	20	19	16	3	J	55
Aft.	7	3	9	11	13	37	9	9	2	J	59
Eve.					[No data]					A	63
AUTUMN											
Morn.	15	9	6	6	8	20	17	18	2	S	61
Aft.	11	9	8	8	11	26	12	12	4	O	57
Eve.					[No data]					N	54

South Coast of England: Sussex and Kent (see Map 1)

GENERAL FEATURES

Because of the fact that it has a wide coastal plain backed by the South Downs for a large part of its length (Chichester Harbour to Beachy Head) and faces the late morning sun, this coast has one of the strongest seabreeze regimes in Britain. The coast beyond Eastbourne is largely flat except for odd outcrops of high ground at Hastings etc. and inland here and down into Kent there is the backbone of the North Downs. Many beaches are sandy – this coast is not known as the South Coast Riviera for nothing, enjoying many hours of unbroken sunshine when the seabreezes blow. Further inland beyond the seabreeze fronts it will often be cloudy but the coast is sheltered from northerlies and so is warm.

MAJOR WINDS

The main trend of the summer wind is to come up the Channel from SW, but having said that wherever there are promontories such as Selsey Bill at one end or Dungeness at the other local oddities will crop up. However, on maybe as many as half the days of late spring and summer of a good year there will be seabreeze fronts forming and moving inland to bring in gentle to moderate afternoon winds over the coasts and the harbours and estuaries. They will also bring periods of calm in the mornings on the coast and during the afternoon or even the evening further inland. Those who sail on inland waters such as Frensham Pond in Surrey may well have to contend with very little wind in the afternoon when they should have maximum wind (see Mistral-seabreeze effect, page 137). On occasional good days of May or June the seabreeze front can still be found creeping on over the Thames some fifty or more miles inland – and after dark!

The Royal Sovereign Light Vessel off Beachy Head gives a good indication of what to expect on this coast in summer:

WINDS (% FREQUENCY) AND SEA TEMPERATURES AT THE ROYAL SOVEREIGN LIGHT VESSEL

	N	NE	E	SE	S	SW	W	NW	Calm	Sea temperatures (°F)
SUMMER										
Down.	8	18	9	4	8	22	15	15	1	Similar to Dungeness
Eve.	2	6	17	4	5	40	20	2	1	(see below)

In the early morning there are winds from NE sinking off the land, but they do not measure up to the westerlies that make up over half the winds that blow at this time, with the most likely direction being SW. By the afternoon that SW trend has been reinforced by the seabreeze forces so that 60% of all winds are from SW or S, and again SW is pre-eminent. This great SW trend is due to (a) the set of the English Channel; (b) the seabreeze forces by day; and (c) the monsoon effect that goes on day and night. Further down the coast in Kent there is the promontory of Dungeness:

WINDS (% FREQUENCY) AND SEA TEMPERATURES AT DUNGENESS

	N	NE	E	SE	S	SW	W	NW	Calm	Sea temperatures (°F)
SPRING										
Morn.	2	12	18	9	8	9	19	11	13	M 44
Aft.	0	6	22	12	7	9	32	6	5	A 46
Eve.				[No data]						M 50
SUMMER										
Morn.	3	10	15	8	4	5	28	14	14	J 57
Aft.	0	4	14	10	4	8	49	9	2	J 62
Eve.				[No data]						A 64
AUTUMN										
Morn.	2	13	9	7	6	8	22	16	16	S 61
Aft.	0	9	12	8	7	10	32	15	8	O 56
Eve.				[No data]						N 51

Here, because of the lie of the land, the SW tendency further west has been transformed into a W or E trend with W stealing the honours. Here summer afternoons ought, on average, to be westerly one day out of two, but even in the mornings the W wind is the most likely.

East Coast of Southeast England and East Anglia (see Map 3)

GENERAL FEATURES

Kent sticks out to try to reach the Continental shore but only nearly makes it at Dover where there are twenty miles separating the coasts. Going north from Dover Strait the North Sea widens. There is the great bight which is the Thames Estuary and then the myriad creeks of Essex and Suffolk before the largely featureless coast of East Anglia runs up to Yarmouth and round to the Wash.

MAJOR WINDS

This is the second strongest seabreeze coast after the South Coast. The main seabreeze current across Kent may well be drawn in to feed the East Anglian one across the Thames Estuary. It is a coast protected from the prevailing westerlies but the sea temperatures tend to be low in spring.

WINDS AND SEA TEMPERATURES AT SHOEBURYNESS

	Calm	Force 1-4	Force 5-6	Force 7+	Sea temperatures (°F)		Remarks
SPRING							The low land of Shoeburyness shows the trends in the Thames Estuary area. The SW trend shown on the Sussex coast extends across to here but most moderate winds are from easterly points on spring afternoons. By summer, while the easterly seabreeze effect is still there so also is the larger SW trend which is the breeze from the South Coast reinforcing the breeze onto the East Coast. This hangs on into summer evenings. There is a fair proportion of fresh to strong winds.
Morn.	Occ.	All	All (n/e/w) (2)	E	M	42	
Aft.	Few	E/SW	NW-E/E-NE (4)	—	A	45	
Eve.	Occ.	All	SW-E/NW (2)	SW	M	52	
SUMMER							
Morn.	Few	All (se)	NW/SW/NE (1)	—	J	56	
Aft.	Few	SW/E	SW-S/NE (2)	—	J	60	
Eve.	Occ.	SW-S	SW-S (1)	—	A	63	
AUTUMN							
Morn.	Occ.	All	All (n) (4)	SW	S	59	
Aft.	Occ.	All	SW-S/NW (3)	—,	O	56	
Eve.	Occ.	All	W-S (3)	SW (1)	N	52	

WINDS (% FREQUENCY) AND SEA TEMPERATURES AT GREAT YARMOUTH (GORLESTON)

	N	NE	E	SE	S	SW	W	NW	Calm	Sea temperatures (°F)		Remarks
SPRING												Gorleston is right on the shore of the open, often bleak coast of East Anglia. There are no very definite trends on this coast. There are seabreezes in summer but other winds are almost as likely. It is a coast of shingle shores with some sands, and winds will often be off-shore.
Morn.	12	12	8	8	12	15	17	12	4	M	42	
Aft.	18	14	9	16	12	10	10	9	3	A	44	
Eve.					[No data]					M	49	
SUMMER												
Morn.	7	5	7	8	21	24	13	7	2	J	54	
Aft.	12	13	7	14	13	14	13	9	4	J	59	
Eve.					[No data]					A	60	
AUTUMN												
Morn.	5	7	4	6	11	27	26	11	3	S	59	
Aft.	9	8	6	10	14	22	17	11	3	O	56	
Eve.					[No data]					N	51	

East Coast of England: the Wash to Durham (see Maps 3 and 4)

GENERAL FEATURES

Next to the sea this is a mainly low coast but it is backed by low hills rather akin to the Downs of the South Coast. Only in a few places, notably by the Vale of Pickering north of Scarborough, does high ground come close to the sea. Apart from the Wash the major inroads are those of the Humber and Tees estuaries.

MAJOR WINDS

This coast is sheltered from the prevailing westerlies and also has a strong potential for seabreezes which will run in as far as the Pennines on spring and summer afternoons. Many of these breezes must be established against the opposition of westerly winds and so seabreeze calms will occur in the mornings and again in the evenings of quiet weather.

WINDS (% FREQUENCY) AND SEA TEMPERATURES AT THE MOUTH OF THE HUMBER (SPURN POINT)

	N	NE	E	SE	S	SW	W	NW	Calm	Sea temperatures (°F)	Remarks
SPRING											Spurn Point is pretty exposed to the winds of the North Sea and shows tendencies in spring and summer for seabreezes to blow into the mouth of the Humber from E and SE. Otherwise winds come from all round the clock, especially in spring and autumn.
Morn.	15	12	9	11	11	11	14	14	5	M 42	
Aft.	16	13	15	16	8	9	12	9	3	A 44	
Eve.					[No data]					M 48	
SUMMER											
Morn.	13	8	5	7	10	16	20	17	5	J 54	
Aft.	12	11	12	18	7	12	15	11	3	J 57	
Eve.					[No data]					A 58	
AUTUMN											
Morn.	7	7	7	5	14	19	21	17	3	S 57	
Aft.	10	7	7	10	11	18	19	15	3	O 54	
Eve.					[No data]					N 49	

WINDS (% FREQUENCY) AND SEA TEMPERATURES AT TYNEMOUTH

	N	NE	E	SE	S	SW	W	NW	Calm	Sea temperatures (°F)	Remarks
SPRING											The great gap down which the Tyne flows leads to morning winds from W being by far the most prevalent throughout the year but quite a few of these are reversed into easterly seabreezes by lunchtime. Tynemouth is pretty representative of what to expect on this long northeast coast of England.
Morn.	15	8	7	5	12	15	26	10	2	M 42	
Aft.	20	14	11	15	9	8	18	4	1	A 44	
Eve.					[No data]					M 47	
SUMMER											
Morn.	14	3	4	4	13	19	32	9	2	J 52	
Aft.	16	9	10	19	8	11	25	2	1	J 57	
Eve.					[No data]					A 57	
AUTUMN											
Morn.	5	5	4	3	13	23	36	10	1	S 55	
Aft.	10	7	6	7	14	16	31	8	1	O 53	
Eve.					[No data]					N 49	

Scottish East Coast: Borders to Aberdeen (see Map 4)

GENERAL FEATURES

North of the Tyne the Cheviot Hills come close to the sea to where the coast turns north-facing into the Firth of Forth. From then on the coast is more or less straight and faces roughly southeast until at Fraserburgh it again presents a northerly aspect into the Moray Firth. The coast is mainly backed by the Grampian Mountains and shows aspects of other areas in the lee of high mountains.

MAJOR WINDS

There are few summer gales on this coast but the wind gets strong on many occasions in spring and more so in autumn. Being close to mountains there are calms both in the mornings and later in the day, due to seabreezes stemming from the off-shore winds when they occur.

WINDS AND SEA TEMPERATURES AT EDINBURGH (TURNHOUSE)

	Calm	Force 1–4	Force 5–6	Force 7+	Sea temperatures (°F)	Remarks
SPRING						Turnhouse is the airport for Edinburgh and is backed on the south by the mountains. The shore of the Forth lies a short distance north. So the general run of winds is representative but the calms are not. At the water-side site of Inchkeith the number of calm mornings (or afternoons) is not likely to exceed one to two days in a fortnight. There are some seabreezes in spring and summer but not many. The main trend is for winds to increase from W to SW during the day.
Morn.	Many	All (ne–n)	W-SE (4)	W	M 41	
Aft.	Few	SW/NE	NW-S/NE-E (8)	W-SW (1)	A 43	
Eve.	Occ.	W-SW/NE	All (nw–n) (4)	W-SW	M 47	
SUMMER						
Morn.	Many	SW-W/NE-E (nw–n/s–se)	SW (1)	SW	J 51	
Aft.	Occ.	W-SW/NE-E (n/s–se)	W-S (6)	W	J 54	
Eve.	Occ.	SW/NE (n–ne)	W-S (4)	SW	A 57	
AUTUMN						
Morn.	Many	SW/NE (nw–n/se)	W-S (3)	SW	S 55	
Aft.	Occ.	SW-W (se)	NW-S (7)	SW	O 52	
Eve.	Often	SW-W (nw–n)	W-S (4)	SW	N 49	

WINDS AND SEA TEMPERATURES AT ABERDEEN

	Calm	Force 1–4	Force 5–6	Force 7+	Sea temperatures (°F)	Remarks
SPRING						Aberdeen is well-sheltered and enjoys a remarkable climate for its latitude. It can experience Föhn winds which raise the temperature to unseasonal heights. It has a seabreeze regime that is aided by the proximity of the mountains. This is by no means an unfriendly coast. The great westerly drive found in the Firth of Forth is absent here but there are southerlies instead and in spring the seabreeze effect increases the daytime wind very markedly on quite a number of occasions.
Morn.	Many	All (ne)	S-SE/NW (2)	NW/SE	M 42	
Aft.	Occ.	S-SE	NW-SW-SE (6)	NW/SE	A 43	
Eve.	Occ.	S-SE/NW	NW-SW-SE (3)	SW/SE	M 48	
SUMMER						
Morn.	Many	NW (ne)	SW-S	—	J 52	
Aft.	Occ.	NW/S-SE (3)	NW-S (3)	—	J 55	
Eve.	Occ.	N-NW/SE (s)	NW/S-SE (1)	—	A 58	
AUTUMN						
Morn.	Often	All (n–e)	NW-SW-SE (3)	SW-S	S 54	
Aft.	Occ.	All (ne)	NW-SW-SE (5)	—	O 52	
Eve.	Often	All (ne)	NW-SW-SE (3)	SW	N 49	

Northwest Coast of Scotland: Caithness to Loch Linnie (*see Map 4*)

GENERAL FEATURES

It is impossible to describe in detail this broken and often wild coast. The Atlantic depressions bring a lot of wet and windy weather to this exposed area but there is still a large number of wonderful venues for sailing when the weather is fair. Here are deep lochs which can provide shelter and the Hebridean islands such as Skye and Lewis can be idyllic even if you have to watch the weather carefully for the sudden deteriorations that occur.

MAJOR WINDS

Strong to gale winds are not quite as prevalent in this area as might be otherwise thought, and in spring there is a trend to winds from SE as well as the more likely westerlies. However, anyone who sails up here on a holiday should treat the weather with respect as we shall see when we look at the relatively sheltered Stornoway on Lewis.

NOTES

Conditions around the islands and in the lochs will be greatly influenced by the proximity of the mountains. There will be channelling of winds along waterways and often this leads to wild water when the strong tidal streams and races oppose the wind.

WINDS AND SEA TEMPERATURES AT STORNOWAY

	Calm	Force 1-4	Force 5-6	Force 7+	Sea temperatures (°F)	Remarks
SPRING						During the middle of the day there are very few winds in the light bracket at Stornoway – and do not forget it is sheltered. There is an increase in moderate winds from S on summer days as well as from NE. Both show some sea-breeze influences but the strong winds predominate. In the local sea area there are more gales at any time of year than these statistics show. On the coasts facing Lewis the wind will be that much stronger.
Morn.	Occ.	SW-SE	All (ne) (8)	S	M 45	
Aft.	Few	SW-SE	All (ne) (15)	W-S (1)	A 46	
Eve.	Few	S/NE	All (ne-se) (11)	W-S	M 50	
SUMMER						
Morn.	Occ.	SW-S	All (e) (4)	W-S (1)	J 52	
Aft.	Few	S/NE	All (e-se) (9)	—	J 55	
Eve.	Few	S/NE	All (se) (7)	S	A 56	
AUTUMN						
Morn.	Occ.	SW-S	All (ne) (12)	All (e-se) (1)	S 55	
Aft.	Few	SW-S	All (nw-w/ne) (15)	NW-S (2)	O 53	
Eve.	Occ.	SW (s)	All (e) (11)	NW-SW-SE (1)	N 51	

WINDS AND SEA TEMPERATURES AT TIREE

	Calm	Force 1-4	Force 5-6	Force 7+	Sea temperatures (°F)	Remarks
SPRING						Tiree is the southernmost of the Inner Hebridean islands and the observing station is again on the sheltered side of the island. Thus the winds opposite are representative of sheltered (i.e. eastern) sides of the islands of the lochs. There are more fresh to strong winds here even than on Lewis but winds from between S and NW predominate. All the things said about keeping an eye on the weather apply here also.
Morn.	Occ.	All	All (ne-e) (14)	W-SE/N (1)	M 45	
Aft.	Few	All	All (ne-e) (17)	NW-SW/SE (1)	A 46	
Eve.	Occ.	All	All (15)	NW-SW/E-SE (1)	M 49	
SUMMER						
Morn.	Occ.	All (e)	N-W/S-SE (6)	NW	J 52	
Aft.	Few	All (e)	All (ne-e) (7)	NW/SW (1)	J 56	
Eve.	Occ.	All (ne)	All (ne-e) (7)	W-SE/NE	A 57	
AUTUMN						
Morn.	Occ.	All (e)	All (18)	NW-SW-SE (2)	S 56	
Aft.	Few	All	All (20)	NW-SW-SE (2)	O 54	
Eve.	Occ.	All	All (ne) (18)	NW-SW-SE (2)	N 51	

Southwest Coast of Scotland and Northwest Coast of England: Firth of Clyde to the Mersey (see Maps 4 and 5)

GENERAL FEATURES

After the highlands and islands of the west coast of Scotland the mountains pull back where the Clyde flows out past Glasgow and apart from occasional outcrops this is the pattern round the Galloway Peninsula and into the Solway Firth which divides Scotland from England. The mountains of Cumbria and the Lake District come closer to the sea but then the foothills of the Pennines pull a long way back to give way eventually to the Cheshire Plain.

MAJOR WINDS

Through the North Channel and into the Irish Sea some shelter from the Atlantic westerlies is to be found and there are unspoiled beaches to be found also. Seabreezes are local and fragmented until you get to the Lancashire coast which becomes a seabreeze-landbreeze window – about the only one on the English west coast.

NOTES

On the shores of Liverpool Bay it is found that winds off the sea (W-NW) amount to 60 per cent of all winds on summer afternoons when winds from landward (E-SE) are fewest. At around dawn the reverse is true with land winds making up 40 per cent of the winds at this time and sea winds being at their lowest frequency. This is because of the coastal plain – it will not be found further north near to the mountains.

WINDS AND SEA TEMPERATURES AT PRESTWICK

	Calm	Force 1-4	Force 5-6	Force 7+	Sea temperatures (°F)	Remarks
SPRING						Prestwick is an airfield facing out across the Firth of Clyde to Arran and beyond it, Mull. This is an area where there is not much sign of many mountain winds but there is a strong swing to seaward of moderate winds on spring and summer afternoons which hangs on into autumn because the inland heights see the direct sun late in the day. There are far less strong to gale winds on such bits of coast than would appear from the offshore islands.
Morn.	Occ.	All (n)	W-S/E-NE (2)	NW	M 43	
Aft.	Few	SW-W	All (n) (6)	–	A 45	
Eve.	Few	All (n/se)	All (n) (3)	–	M 51	
SUMMER						
Morn.	Occ.	All (n)	W-NW (1)	–	J 53	
Aft.	Few	W-SW (n)	NW-SW/E-NE (2)	–	J 55	
Eve.	Few	SW-NW (n)	NW-S (2)	–	A 56	
AUTUMN						
Morn.	Occ.	All (n)	All (n-ne) (3)	SW/NW	S 56	
Aft.	Occ.	SW	NW-S/NE (5)	NW/SE/NE	O 54	
Eve.	Occ.	All	NW-SW/E-SE (4)	W/E	N 52	

WINDS AND SEA TEMPERATURES AT LIVERPOOL (SPEKE)

	Calm	Force 1-4	Force 5-6	Force 7+	Sea temperatures (°F)	Remarks
SPRING						The lighter wind directions at Liverpool's airport owe a lot to the Mersey that flows closely by. This channels the seabreeze and means a preponderance of gentle or moderate winds from NW on spring and summer afternoons and evenings. Out on the coast there is a problem because in Liverpool Bay the beach shelves so slightly that the water floods and recedes at a rapid rate and leaves you high and dry before you have a chance to have a decent sail.
Morn.	Occ.	All	W-SW/SE (4)	–	M 42	
Aft.	Occ.	All (n)	NW-SW/SE (8)	W-SW	A 44	
Eve.	Few	NW	All (n-se) (4)	SW	M 52	
SUMMER						
Morn.	Occ.	All	NW-S (2)	–	J 55	
Aft.	Few	NW-W (ne)	NW-SW (5)	–	J 60	
Eve.	Occ.	NW	NW-S (4)	W-S	A 61	
AUTUMN						
Morn.	Occ.	All	NW-SW (4)	SW	S 59	
Aft.	Occ.	S (ne)	All (n-e) (7)	NW/SW (1)	O 55	
Eve.	Occ.	All	All (n-e)(5)	–	N 48	

The Coasts of Wales (see Map 5)

GENERAL FEATURES

Wales sticks out from England as a roughly square chunk of mountainous terrain. The mountains are often close to the coast. There are some good sailing shores here, and on the north and south coasts shelter from the prevailing westerlies.

MAJOR WINDS

The main sea wind will come up St George's Channel from SW and there can be some very high seas in the Irish Sea. Local seabreezes will often occur and in many cases will reinforce an already on-shore wind which will raise its speed into the fresh bracket. The local winds will be very much altered by the topography especially when it is either very hot or (in winter) very cold.

WINDS AND SEA TEMPERATURES AT ANGLESEY (VALLEY)

	Calm	Force 1–4	Force 5–6	Force 7+	Sea temperatures (°F)	Remarks
SPRING						Valley is an airfield on the coast of Anglesey facing the Irish Sea. It represents the coasts that are exposed to the Irish Sea winds. The Menai Straits between Anglesey and the mainland can be a dangerous place both for wind and tide but there is good sailing to be had on the north Welsh (holiday resort) coast. Cardigan Bay is exposed but has some good beaches and there is shelter in some of the coves.
Morn.	Often	All	All (n–ne) (8)	W–S (1)	M 44	
Aft.	Few	S–SW	All (n/e) (11)	SW–S (1)	A 47	
Eve.	Occ.	SW/NE	All (w–n)	SW–S (1)	M 49	
SUMMER						
Morn.	Often	SW (e)	NW–S (7)	SW	J 54	
Aft.	Few	SW–NW (e)	NW–S (7)	SW–S	J 58	
Eve.	Occ.	SW (se–e)	NW–S (8)	SW	A 60	
AUTUMN						
Morn.	Occ.	SW/NW	All (e) (13)	NW–SW (2)	S 59	
Aft.	Occ.	S–SW/NW	All (ne/se) (15)	W–SW	O 55	
Eve.	Occ.	All	All (n) (15)	W–SW (2)	N 52	

WINDS AND SEA TEMPERATURES AT CARDIFF (PENNYLAN)

	Calm	Force 1–4	Force 5–6	Force 7+	Sea temperatures (°F)	Remarks
SPRING						The airport of Pennylan lies close to the water on the north side of the Bristol Channel. It is a perfect example of channelled winds for we find that most of the time the winds are either W or E and on spring and summer afternoons and evenings approaching half the winds are from W. Despite that, it has few gales but quite a high proportion of fresh to strong winds. Westwards out to Milford Haven there are many rocky and sandy beaches but further into the Severn Estuary there is a very large tidal range and great areas dry at low water.
Morn.	Occ.	All (n)	W/E (4)	W–NW	M 47	
Aft.	Few	W (n)	W (9)	W	A 48	
Eve.	Occ.	W (n)	W/E (6)	W	M 54	
SUMMER						
Morn.	Occ.	All (n)	W/E (3)	W/E	J 60	
Aft.	Few	W (n)	W (6)	W	J 63	
Eve.	Few	W (n)	W (5)	—	A 61	
AUTUMN						
Morn.	Occ.	All (n)	W–S (4)	W–S (1)	S 59	
Aft.	Few	All	W (6)	W–SW (1)	O 55	
Eve.	Occ.	All	W/S–SE (4)	W–SW (1)	N 52	

Bristol Channel to Isles of Scilly

(see Maps 1 and 5)

GENERAL FEATURES

The mouth of the Severn is a natural funnel that generates a big tidal bore that needs careful study if you intend to sail within its throw. The north coasts of Avon and Devon are backed by the Mendip Hills and Exmoor. Neither are very high but they serve to channel the winds west–east along these shores. From Barnstaple down to Land's End much of the coast is high and rocky but it is here that the surfers find substitutes for the Pacific rollers.

MAJOR WINDS

This is an exposed coast for much of its length and so there are a fair proportion of strong winds. These are often reinforced by the seabreezes that blow towards Bodmin Moor and Dartmoor. The Scilly Isles themselves are not beyond the throw of this summer drive towards the land.

WINDS AND SEA TEMPERATURES AT ST MAWGAN

	Calm	Force 1–4	Force 5–6	Force 7+	Sea temperatures (°F)	Remarks
SPRING						St Mawgan is at 337 ft, quite high up so it will be fairly representative of the winds that blow in off the sea onto the exposed beaches of West Cornwall. When the winds blow off the land, however, those some beaches will be well sheltered so a wide range of conditions are to be found. The summer afternoons and evenings find a good number of seabreezes blowing.
Morn.	Occ.	All	All (n-ne) (7)	NW/SE (1)	M 47	
Aft.	Few	W/N	All (n-ne) (13)	W/SE	A 48	
Eve.	Few	W/N	All (n-e) (9)	SE	M 51	
SUMMER						
Morn.	Occ.	All	NW-W/S (3)	NW	J 59	
Aft.	Few	W-NW (e-ne)	NW-S (6)	SE	J 60	
Eve.	Few	W-N (e-ne)	NW-SW (4)	—	A 60	
AUTUMN						
Morn.	Occ.	All	NW-S (9)	NW-SW	S 59	
Aft.	Few	All	All (n-e) (11)	NW-SW/SE (1)	O 57	
Eve.	Occ.	All	All (n-e) (8)	NW-SW/SE (1)	N 53	

WINDS AND SEA TEMPERATURES AT ST MARY'S, SCILLY

	Calm	Force 1–4	Force 5–6	Force 7+	Sea temperatures (°F)	Remarks
SPRING						This complex of small islands are not called the 'Fortunate Isles' for nothing and have some very pleasant beaches and bays. It is most likely that the islands will be swept by a W breeze that owes its origin to the collective breezes blowing onto the coasts of Cornwall as well as those further into the English Channel. There are very few gales in summer despite the exposed position.
Morn.	Occ.	All	NW-W (6)	NW-W/S (1)	M 49	
Aft.	Occ.	All	SW-SE (12)	NW-W (1)	A 50	
Eve.	Occ.	All	NW/SW (11)	NW-SW (1)	M 53	
SUMMER						
Morn.	Occ.	All	W-NW (3)	NW	J 59	
Aft.	Occ.	W (e-se)	W-NW (3)	W-NW	J 60	
Eve.	Occ.	W-NW (e)	W (4)	W-NW	A 62	
AUTUMN						
Morn.	Occ.	All (ne)	W-NW/NE (12)	All (s-e) (12)	S 61	
Aft.	Occ.	All	W (14)	SW-N (2)	O 57	
Eve.	Occ.	All	W (13)	SW-N (2)	N 53	

Irish West and North Coasts (*see Map 6*)

GENERAL FEATURES

The southwest tip of Ireland is like the west coast of Scotland – mountain and loch. Then it is bays, many of them quite large like Galway and Clew Bays, and there is the long Shannon Estuary north of Killarney. There are always isolated groups of mountains, and when we get to Donegal these come down to the sea and this continues round the top of Ireland into Lough Foyle. There are many inland loughs that will give good sailing – and far from the madding crowd at that!

MAJOR WINDS

Even though it faces the unfettered Atlantic this coast is not as wild as one might suppose. Only in autumn do the gales at sea reach as much as twenty-four hours in a fortnight. In summer there is a mere chance of four hours in a fortnight, and then only from W. There is plenty of variation in this coast to allow finding delightful beaches and sheltered sailing.

WINDS AND SEA TEMPERATURES AT SHANNON

	Calm	Force 1-4	Force 5-6	Force 7+	Sea temperatures (°F)	Remarks
SPRING						Shannon Airport lies so far inland from the sea that it is representative of inland sailing, being on the edge of a tidal lake. No Force 7 winds make the statistics so there are very few of them. The seabreeze comes in strongly on summer days but winds from NE are rare. If you do get a great deal of wind when you do not want it then you are just unlucky.
Morn.	Occ.	All	SW-SE (3)	W	M 49	
Aft.	Few	All (n-ne)	All (n-e) (10)	W	A 49	
Eve.	Few	All	W-SW (4)	SW-SE	M 52	
SUMMER						
Morn.	Occ.	All (ne)	W-SW (1)	SW	J 56	
Aft.	Few	NW-SW (ne)	W-SW (4)	SW	J 59	
Eve.	Few	W-NW (e-ne)	W-SW (2)	—	A 60	
AUTUMN						
Morn.	Few	All	W-SE (4)	SW	S 57	
Aft.	Few	SW (ne)	W-SW (6)	SW	O 55	
Eve.	Few	All	W-S (5)	W-SW	N 53	

WINDS AND SEA TEMPERATURES AT BELMULLET

	Calm	Force 1-4	Force 5-6	Force 7+	Sea temperatures (°F)	Remarks
SPRING						Belmullet is on the island that forms the end of the Mullet Peninsula. It is the extreme northwest corner of Ireland. It is a lot windier up here than further south. Even so, Belmullet is on the sheltered side of the island so on exposed coasts the winds will be stronger. The big summer directions are W to SW and as they grow with the day, many are seabreezes.
Morn.	Few	All (n)	W-S (10)	SW-S/NW (1)	M 48	
Aft.	Few	All (n/e)	W-S (17)	NW-SW (1)	A 49	
Eve.	Few	All	W-SW (10)	W-S (1)	M 52	
SUMMER						
Morn.	Occ.	W-SW (se)	W-S (5)	—	J 55	
Aft.	Few	NW-SW (n)	W-S (10)	—	J 57	
Eve.	Few	SW-W (e)	W-S (7)	—	A 59	
AUTUMN						
Morn.	Occ.	SW (n/s)	W-SW (11)	All (e-se) (1)	S 57	
Aft.	Few	SW-S (n)	W-S (14)	NW-S (1)	O 55	
Eve.	Occ.	SW (n)	W-S (12)	NW-S (1)	N 53	

Irish East and South Coasts (see Map 6)

GENERAL FEATURES

At the northern end surrounding Belfast where the coast looks across the relatively narrow North Channel to Scotland there are the Antrim Mountains on the north side and Belfast and Strangford Loughs on the other. Then the coast is generally lower indented by bay and estuary until one reaches the Wicklow Mountains. Around Wexford in the southeast corner the land is again low but right along the south coast to the Fastnet Rock the high ground is never very far from the sea.

MAJOR WINDS

The Irish Sea and the Fastnet sea area are well known for their occasionally ferocious storms but on the whole the Irish Sea coast is sheltered. Much shelter can also be found in the bays and inlets on the south coast.

NOTES

Offshore gales in spring come from between SW and NE through NW and amount to some 12 hours in an average fortnight. In summer they are mainly from NW and are four times less frequent, while in autumn they come from round the clock at rather less frequency than in spring.

WINDS AND SEA TEMPERATURES AT DUBLIN

	Calm	Force 1–4	Force 5–6	Force 7+	Sea temperatures (°F)	Remarks
SPRING						Obviously from the number of dashes in the Force 7+ column Dublin is, like so many places on this coast, well sheltered from the stronger winds. Seabreezes do not get frequent or strong on this coast because of the hunger of the mainland coasts opposite for the available Irish Sea air. Thus westerlies increase with the day in all three seasons. When winds blow on-shore they can be fresh.
Morn.	Occ.	SE (n/s)	W–SW (2)	—	M 46	
Aft.	Few	W/SE (n)	NW–SW/SE (7)	—	A 47	
Eve.	Few	SW (n)	NW–SW/E–NE (3)	—	M 50	
SUMMER						
Morn.	Occ.	W–SW (ne)	W–SW (1)	—	J 54	
Aft.	Few	NW–SW (s)	NW–SW (2)	—	J 56	
Eve.	Few	W(s)	W–SW (1)	—	A 59	
AUTUMN						
Morn.	Occ.	W–SW (n)	W–SW/SE (3)	—	S 57	
Aft.	Few	W–SW (n)	NW–SW/SE–E (5)	—	O 55	
Eve.	Few	W–SW (n)	W–SW/SE (2)	—	N 52	

WINDS (% FREQUENCY) AND SEA TEMPERATURES AT ROCHE POINT

	N	NE	E	SE	S	SW	W	NW	Calm	Sea temperatures (°F)	Remarks
SPRING											Roche Point is at the entrance to Cork Harbour in the centre of the south coast. It is hardly ever calm, although the harbour can be. There are strong swings to SW in summer and autumn showing that this coast gets better seabreezes than the Irish Sea one does. There are quite strong trends towards having winds sinking off the Boggeragh Mountains inland.
Morn.	30	7	6	15	3	17	11	12	0	M 48	
Aft.	17	5	7	21	6	23	8	11	0	A 49	
Eve.					[No data]					M 52	
SUMMER											
Morn.	30	1	3	9	3	24	12	18	0	J 56	
Aft.	16	1	1	15	4	40	9	15	0	J 59	
Eve.					[No data]					A 60	
AUTUMN											
Morn.	27	8	3	8	2	21	19	14	0	S 58	
Aft.	16	4	3	12	4	35	14	16	0	O 56	
Eve.					[No data]					N 52	

Belgium and Holland: Dunkerque to Texel (see Map 7)

GENERAL FEATURES

This is a low coast and faces the prevailing winds. There are two long runs of straight coastline (a) from Dunkerque to the Westerschelde and (b) from the Hook of Holland to Den Helder. Between these are the immensely convoluted waters of the Schelde estuary. To the north the Noord Holland is a tongue of land across which the winds can blow without interference, crossing the Ijsselmeer and on into the heart of the Netherlands and Germany.

MAJOR WINDS

There are more calms than one might expect on these coasts but nevertheless the major trend is to have winds of all speeds from SW as the major direction (including gales). These will be enhanced by having to blow side-shore along the Belgian coast. NW is another strong wind direction in summer and autumn but there can also be strong NE winds, i.e. off-shore and so potentially dangerous.

WINDS AND SEA TEMPERATURES AT OSTEND

	Calm	Force 1-4	Force 5-6	Force 7+	Sea temperatures (°F)	Remarks
SPRING						This is a very windy coast with the westerly winds predominating but there is a strong trend to either blow up the coast from SW or down it from NE. Throughout the seasons there are sea-breezes from W which frequently reinforce the already on-shore winds to blow up to Force 7 or more. The contrast with the English coast opposite could not be more marked. Here is a sailboarder's coast with a fair chance of side-shore strong winds.
Mom.	Few	SW	SW-W/N-NE (8)	SW-W	M 42	
Aft.	Few	W-SW/NE-N (9e)	W-SW/N-NE (11)	W-SW/ N-NE (1)	A 46	
Eve.	Few	W/NE (9e)	W-SW/N-NE (14)	W-SW/ NE-E (1)	M 52	
SUMMER						
Mom.	Few	SW-NW	SW-NW/NE (7)	W-SW (1)	J 57	
Aft.	Few	W (e)	SW-NW (11)	SW-NW/ NE (1)	J 62	
Eve.	Few	SW	All (s-ne) (12)	SW-NW/ NE (1)	A 64	
AUTUMN						
Mom.	Few	SW	SW-NW/E (9)	SW-NW (1)	S 61	
Aft.	Few	W/NE (s-se)	All (s-e) (14)	All (s-se) (1)	O 57	
Eve.	Few	All	All (s-e) (12)	All (s-e) (1)	N 50	

WINDS AND SEA TEMPERATURES AT VLISSINGEN (FLUSHING)

	Calm	Force 1-4	Force 5-6	Force 7+	Sea temperatures (°F)	Remarks
SPRING						Vlissingen lies on the south coast of the island of Walcheren. It is windier than further into the Zeeland complex but it shows (compared to Ostend and Den Helder) what a little shelter can do. Even so there is still quite a lot of wind and the NE trend at Ostend has become a northerly here. Over half the summer afternoons have westerly seabreezes. However, the very few calms, when the winds were recorded only 18 ft above sea level, shows that there is always going to be wind of some sort.
Mom.	Few	All	W-S (4)	W	M 43	
Aft.	Few	W/N (s)	W-SW (6)	W	A 45	
Eve.	Few	N (s)	W-SW (4)	W-SW (1)	M 53	
SUMMER						
Mom.	Few	SW-W	SW-S (2)	—	J 57	
Aft.	Few	W (9s)	W-SW (4)	SW	J 63	
Eve.	Occ.	W-SW (e-se)	W-SW (3)	—	A 64	
AUTUMN						
Mom.	Few	S-SW (n)	W-S (5)	S	S 62	
Aft.	Few	S-W	SW-S (7)	SW-S	O 56	
Eve.	Occ.	All	W-S (4)	SW	N 49	

The Frisian Coast – Helgoland Bight
(see Map 7)

GENERAL FEATURES

From the island of Texel up round the shoulder of the Netherlands and right along the north German coast of Harlingerland lies the string of islands called the Frisians. There is much sport to be had here and a great deal of wind as well. Only in the shelter of the Ems and Weser estuaries will the strength of the westerlies be broken. Up the west-facing coast of Germany there are the North Frisians but the whole coast tends to be low.

MAJOR WINDS

There is a phenomenon in this area which is like a summer 'monsoon'. Winds are fed in a corridor of increased westerly frequency across the waist of the Danish peninsula and on up the Ostsee and into the Baltic. This supplies the great seabreeze feed onto all these Baltic coasts from Germany and Sweden to Finland and Russia. Thus the W trend is strong here.

NOTES

Winds offshore in the Helgoland Bight have a trend to come from W or SW in summer but while SW gales are known they are not frequent. The gales in spring come mainly from SW or NE and amount to an average three hours in a four-day period. The chances of such winds are the same in autumn but then, as well as SW, there are NW and SE gales.

WINDS AND SEA TEMPERATURES AT DEN HELDER

	Calm	Force 1–4	Force 5–6	Force 7+	Sea temperatures (°F)	Remarks
SPRING						Den Helder is the windiest place in the North Sea for which we have statistics. Some of this strength might be due to funnelling through the Schulpengat between Den Helder and Texel. Even so the predominant wind direction at any time is SW and this becomes a more than even chance in summer. Yet round the corner into the East Frisians there is also a trend to easterly winds during spring and summer.
Mom.	Few	All	All (se) (14)	W–S/ E–NE (1)	M 40	
Aft.	Few	SW (se)	All (se–e) (19)	N–E (1)	A 45	
Eve.	Few	SW/N (se)	All (se) (16)	W–NW (1)	M 53	
SUMMER						
Mom.	Few	SW–W (se)	All (e–se) (12)	W–SW	J 58	
Aft.	Few	SW–NW (se)	All (se–e) (15)	SW	J 62	
Eve.	Few	SW (se)	All (e–se) (12)	SW (1)	A 64	
AUTUMN						
Mom.	Few	All	All (s–se) (15)	NW–S (1)	S 62	
Aft.	Few	W–S (se)	All (s–se) (19)	W–S (1)	O 56	
Eve.	Few	All	All (se) (16)	All (se–ne) (1)	N 50	

WINDS AND SEA TEMPERATURES AT WESTERLAND (SYLT)

	Calm	Force 1–4	Force 5–6	Force 7+	Sea temperatures (°F)	Remarks
SPRING						It is very noticeable that the SW–W 'monsoon' tendency has died out up here on Sylt. There is still a fair chance of wind compared to many other places but it is not as likely that you will get Force 5 in the North Frisians as in the East Frisians. There is a north-westerly seabreeze in spring and summer, but the afternoon breeze may also come from W or SW.
Mom.	Occ.	SE–NE	SE–NW/W–NW (4)	—	M 38	
Aft.	Few	NW (ne)	W–N/E–S (6)	—	A 42	
Eve.	Few	NW/E (s)	All (s/n) (5)	—	M 49	
SUMMER						
Mom.	Occ.	NW (s)	SW–N (2)	—	J 55	
Aft.	Few	NW–SW (ne)	All (ne) (2)	—	J 61	
Eve.	Few	NW–SW (ne)	NW/SW/E (2)	—	A 62	
AUTUMN						
Mom.	Occ.	SE (ne)	All (s/ne) (5)	SW	S 59	
Aft.	Few	SW–SE (n)	All (n) (5)	SW–S/ NW (1)	O 55	
Eve.	Occ.	All	All (6)	NW (1)	N 48	

Danish West Coast (*see Map 8*)

GENERAL FEATURES

From the North Frisian islands the coast runs straight northwards to where the Lim Fjord cuts off the extreme north of Denmark from the rest. It is a low coast bitten into half way up by Ringkøbing Fjorden. The coast facing the Skagerrak looks northwestwards and ends in Skagens Rev.

MAJOR WINDS

It is still very windy on these coasts as they face the open North Sea. The westerly trend continues but with the land masses of Denmark and Sweden pulling in increasing winds from between W and NW in the summer. There are some calms but on the whole the picture is that your chances of some strong daytime winds is high.

WINDS AND SEA TEMPERATURES AT VESTERVIG

	Calm	Force 1–4	Force 5–6	Force 7+	Sea temperatures (°F)	Remarks
SPRING						In the summer mornings Vestervig shows that there are many gentle to moderate winds before the sun is really up as there will be in the afternoon. The winds tend to go down and shift direction in the evenings. However, at all times and in all seasons there are W to SW winds predominating. Really strong winds tend to blow up in the mornings and the evenings in summer.
Morn.	Few	W–SW (n)	W/E (5)	NW	M 38	
Aft.	Few	NW–SW (n)	SW/E (7)	NW–SW (1)	A 42	
Eve.	Few	All (n)	W/E (5)	SW	M 48	
SUMMER						
Morn.	Few	W–SW (n)	NW–SW (3)	W	J 56	
Aft.	Few	W–SW	W–NW (4)	W	J 60	
Eve.	Few	W (n–ne)	W (4)	W–SW (1)	A 61	
AUTUMN						
Morn.	Few	All (n)	W–NW/SE (8)	NW–SW (2)	S 58	
Aft.	Few	W–SW (n)	W–NW/E (8)	NW–SW (1)	O 53	
Eve.	Few	All (n)	All (n–e) (8)	W–NW (1)	N 45	

WINDS AND SEA TEMPERATURES AT SKAGENS REV

	Calm	Force 1–4	Force 5–6	Force 7+	Sea temperatures (°F)	Remarks
SPRING						Skagens Rev is a lightvessel on the tip of Denmark where the Skagerrak and the Kattegat divide. There is always wind along this coast but only in summer are there any real trends to have increasing westerlies with the day.
Morn.	Few	All	W–SW/E–NE (6)	W–NW (1)	M 37	
Aft.	Few	All	W–SW/E–NE (5)	W–NW (1)	A 41	
Eve.	Few	All	SW–S/N (5)	W–NW (1)	M 48	
SUMMER						
Morn.	Few	W–SW (n)	W–S (5)	W–NW (1)	J 57	
Aft.	Few	W (ne)	W–SW (4)	W/N	J 61	
Eve.	Few	W (nw–ne)	W–SW (6)	W (1)	A 62	
AUTUMN						
Morn.	Few	All	All (nw–n)	W–S (2)	S 58	
Aft.	Few	All	All (e)	W–NE (2)	O 54	
Eve.	Few	All	All (n) (14)	W–S (1)	N 46	

The Kattegat and Danish Archipelago
(see Map 8)

GENERAL FEATURES

On the Swedish side of the Kattegat the coast is rather broken but a useful coastal plain exists before the ground begins to rise. The winds of this coast are going to be like Skagens Rev but with more calms and more seabreezes by day and winds off the land by night. The complex of islands that make up so much of the land mass of Denmark have so many features that it is impossible to describe them in detail.

MAJOR WINDS

There is a great deal of shelter in these waters for over 50 per cent of the winds are Force 1–3 at Anholt Fyr in the middle of the Kattegat in spring and summer and only half this number are Force 4–5. The W–SW trend is still there though overriding the tendencies to blow along the waterways.

WINDS AND SEA TEMPERATURES AT ODENSE

	Calm	Force 1–4	Force 5–6	Force 7+	Sea temperatures (°F)	Remarks
SPRING						Odense is on the island of Fyn and is representative of the northern parts of the archipelago. There is a strong seabreeze pull onto the Swedish shores in summer but this tends to increase the winds that are already blowing moderately from W or SW in the mornings. Many seabreezes go calm on summer evenings but the fresh winds are still to be found at this time of day.
Morn.	Occ.	All	W/E (5)	SW	M 37	
Aft.	Few	All	W-SW/NE (14)	W-SW (1)	A 41	
Eve.	Occ.	All (n-nw)	W-SW/E (6)	W-SW (1)	M 48	
SUMMER						
Morn.	Occ.	SW-W (n)	W (3)	—	J 56	
Aft.	Few	SW-W	W-SE (10)	W-S	J 62	
Eve.	Often	SW (nw)	W-S (4)	—	A 62	
AUTUMN						
Morn.	Occ.	W-SW (nw-n)	W-SW (5)	—	S 58	
Aft.	Few	All (nw)	W-SW/E (11)	W-SW (1)	O 54	
Eve.	Occ.	All (nw-n)	SW-S (7)	W-S (1)	N 46	

WINDS AND SEA TEMPERATURES AT GEDSER REV

	Calm	Force 1–4	Force 5–6	Force 7+	Sea temperatures (°F)	Remarks
SPRING						Gedser Rev is at the lowest extremity of the group of Danish islands. There are no thermal wind trends to be seen but the summer 'monsoon' blows across here on its way into the Baltic proper. There are going to be seabreezes by day and landbreezes by night but they are going to have to be assessed on the spot if you sail these convoluted waters. Whatever other message Gedser gives it is certainly a relatively windy place.
Morn.	Few	All	All (s-e) (3)	SW-NW (1)	M 36	
Aft.	Occ.	All	SW-N (3)	—	A 40	
Eve.	Occ.	All (n)	W/E (3)	N-NE (1)	M 48	
SUMMER						
Morn.	Few	SW-NW (n)	SW-NW (3)	SW-NW (1)	J 56	
Aft.	Occ.	W (s)	SW-NW (2)	SW-N (1)	J 61	
Eve.	Occ.	W (n/s)	SW-NW (3)	W	A 62	
AUTUMN						
Morn.	Few	SW	NW-S/NE (9)	W-NW (1)	S 58	
Aft.	Few	All	W-SW/NE (10)	W-NW (1)	O 54	
Eve.	Few	All	W-SW/E-SE (9)	NW-SW (1)	N 46	

Eastern Coasts of Sweden (see Map 8)

GENERAL FEATURES

Southern Swedish shores face the Ostsee and so look more or less south but where the Kalmarsund separates the coast on which Kalmar stands from the long finger of the island of Oland the coast runs northwards and becomes very fragmented. Stockholm lies in the middle of a most broken and scattered set of islands and off here the waters are cold and the Baltic pack ice builds up through the winter, only breaking in the spring.

MAJOR WINDS

On the southern coasts the winds will have that SW trend that we have identified as the summer 'monsoon' and which becomes channelled by the shores of the Ostsee. Around the corner there is a great deal of shelter from this strong trend and winds are far more likely to come from any direction. However, on the off-shore islands of Gotland and Maarianhamina there is a massive tendency for the wind to be from S.

WINDS AND SEA TEMPERATURES AT HAMMERHUS (BORNHOLM)

	Calm	Force 1-4	Force 5-6	Force 7+	Sea temperatures (°F)	Remarks
SPRING						Hammerhus on the northern tip of the island of Bornholm shows how the winds blow between the south Swedish shores and the Baltic coasts of Germany and Poland. Throughout the season the major wind directions are SW and NE. However, the former is far more likely and on summer evenings it is almost certain. However, the Swedish coast will haul in the seabreezes when the sun shines.
Morn.	Occ.	All (n)	W/N-NE (2)	E	M 36	
Aft.	Occ.	SW (n)	W/N-E (2)	NE	A 38	
Eve.	Occ.	All (n)	W/N-E (2)	NE	M 45	
SUMMER						
Morn.	Occ.	SW-W (n)	NW-SW/NE (2)	SW	J 54	
Aft.	Occ.	W-SW (n)	W-SW/NE (2)	W	J 61	
Eve.	Occ.	W-SW	NW-SW/NE (2)	—	A 62	
AUTUMN						
Morn.	Occ.	All (s)	NW-SW/NE (5)	NW-SW/NE-E (2)	S 58	
Aft.	Occ.	All	NW-SW/NE-E (1)	NW-SW/NE-E (1)	O 53	
Eve.	Occ.	All	NW-SW (5)	W-NW (1)	N 46	

WINDS AND SEA TEMPERATURES AT MAARIANHAMINA

	Calm	Force 1-4	Force 5-6	Force 7+	Sea temperatures (°F)	Remarks
SPRING						Maarianhamina is on the south side of the island of Ahvenanmaa in the narrow waist between Sweden and Finland. It represents the conditions at the mouth of the Gulf of Bothnia, and is more representative of coastal conditions than Stockholm, which is very sheltered. The trend is for the summer wind to blow almost exclusively from S by day while the same effect is there in spring and to a lesser extent in autumn. This shows that cold Baltic waters are the seat of many seabreezes that must be fed through this narrow waterway. Stockholm is windier but has no real trends in its winds which come from all round the
Morn.	Occ.	All (w)	SW-SE/NW-N (1)	—	M 34	
Aft.	Few	S	S/NW-NE (2)	—	A 34	
Eve.	Occ.	S/N (w/ne)	—	—	M 40	
SUMMER						
Morn.	Occ.	All	NW	—	J 48	
Aft.	Few	S	S-SW/N-NW (1)	—	J 57	
Eve.	Few	S (w/e)	NW	—	A 59	
AUTUMN						
Morn.	Often	All (ne)	S/NW (1)	—	S 54	
Aft.	Few	S (ne)	SW-SE/NW (1)	—	O 48	
Eve.	Often	S (ne)	S-SW/N (1)	—	N 43	

Northwest France: Strait of Dover to Cherbourg (see Map 1)

GENERAL FEATURES

From the narrowest part of La Manche (English Channel) the coast faces west and looks straight down the Channel. There are few natural harbours but many beaches, and the winds will have a very definite on-shore daytime trend in spring and summer. Then beyond Abbeville the coast turns to face northwest before we come to the Baie de la Seine. There are many good beaches here and shelter from the Cherbourg Peninsula if required.

MAJOR WINDS

The main wind to be expected is one off the sea, and in places where there is little shelter it can be a windy coast.

WINDS AND SEA TEMPERATURES AT ABBEVILLE

	Calm	Force 1–4	Force 5–6	Force 7+	Sea temperatures (°F)	Remarks
SPRING						Abbeville is not representative of the Picardy coast as it lies some twelve miles inland, but it shows the way that the wind picks up from morning light airs or calm to a wind from the sea by midday throughout the seasons. Some of these winds get as high as fresh and, allowing for the sheltering effect of the land, this shows that on the coast there will often be a brisk on-shore wind right through into the evening.
Morn.	Often	All	W-SW (1)	—	M 44	
Aft.	Few	W/NE	W-SW (5)	—	A 47	
Eve.	Occ.	W/NE (e-se)	W-SW (2)	W-SW	M 52	
SUMMER						
Morn.	Many	SW-W (e)	—	—	J 57	
Aft.	Occ.	W (e)	W-SW (2)	—	J 62	
Eve.	Occ.	W (se)	W-SW (2)	—	A 64	
AUTUMN						
Morn.	Often	All	NW-SW (1)	—	S 62	
Aft.	Occ.	W-SW	W-SW (2)	—	O 57	
Eve.	Occ.	All	W-NW (1)	—	N 53	

WINDS AND SEA TEMPERATURES AT CAP DE LA HÈVE

	Calm	Force 1–4	Force 5–6	Force 7+	Sea temperatures (°F)	Remarks
SPRING						Up on the cliffs outside Le Havre is Cap de la Hève. This is not representative of the beaches because of its great height (335 ft). However what it shows is that a lot of wind blows up the Channel and so exposed beaches will see some of this force. Yet where there is shelter it will be much quieter. Winds blow quite strongly from NE here as well and beaches around Deauville will see these winds as side-shore ones.
Morn.	Few	E-NE (nw)	W-SW/NE (17)	W-S/ N-NE (1)	M 47	
Aft.	Few	All	All (s-e) (17)	All (s-e) (2)	A 48	
Eve.	Few	NE (se)	W-SW/NE (16)	All (e-se) (3)	M 52	
SUMMER						
Morn.	Occ.	All	All (e-se) (15)	W-SW (2)	J 58	
Aft.	Occ.	NW-SW (se)	NW-SW (14)	W-SW (2)	J 62	
Eve.	Few	W-NE (e-s)	SW-NW/NE (12)	W-SW (2)	A 63	
AUTUMN						
Morn.	Few	All	All (ne-se) (19)	NW-SW (4)	S 62	
Aft.	Few	All	All (ne-se) (19)	All (e-se) (4)	O 57	
Eve.	Few	All	NW-S/NE (18)	NW-SW (2)	N 53	

North Brittany Coast of France
(see Map 1)

GENERAL FEATURES

The coast beyond the Cherbourg Peninsula becomes much more rugged and in the St Malo area there are very great tidal ranges. There are many coves and little bays and down towards Brest a backbone of higher ground lies some way inland from the coast. This coast lies outside the mainstream of Channel winds but develops its own sea-breeze system.

MAJOR WINDS

The winds of this part of the French coast are predominantly either from W–SW or from NE. In the case of the westerlies these pick up with the day, as happens along most north-facing coasts wherever you are. The strongest winds, however, are found when the wind is on-shore from NE, but there are not many, especially in summer.

WINDS AND SEA TEMPERATURES AT CHERBOURG

	Calm	Force 1–4	Force 5–6	Force 7+	Sea temperatures (°F)	Remarks
SPRING						Cherbourg Harbour is a good place to show the way the W to SW wind picks up on this side of the Channel with the day and this trend is there in all three seasons. It is a quirk of the exposure of the wind recorder that makes NE winds appear stronger than W winds but out on the exposed coasts the latter will pick up to Force 7 more often than these statistics show. The Channel Islands will be swept by these winds either up the Channel or down it.
Morn.	Often	All (nw-se)	W/E (4)	NE	M 46	
Aft.	Few	W-SW/NE (se)	W/NE (7)	—	A 49	
Eve.	Occ.	W/NE-E (se)	W/NE (5)	E	M 52	
SUMMER						
Morn.	Many	W-SW (nw/se)	SW/NE (1)	—	J 55	
Aft.	Few	W-SW (s-se)	W/NE (2)	—	J 59	
Eve.	Occ.	W (n/s-se)	W/NE (1)	—	A 61	
AUTUMN						
Morn.	Often	All (se)	W/NE (3)	—	S 61	
Aft.	Occ.	W-SW (se)	W/NE (3)	—	O 57	
Eve.	Occ.	All (se)	W/NE (3)	NE	N 54	

WINDS AND SEA TEMPERATURES AT BREST (GUIPAVAS)

	Calm	Force 1–4	Force 5–6	Force 7+	Sea temperatures (°F)	Remarks
SPRING						Guipavas is an airfield some 15 miles inland from the end of Brittany. The same SW/NE trend in the winds is evident here as it was at Cherbourg showing that these are the prime directions for this coast. There are not many strong winds here but again it will be stronger out on the coasts that face Ushant and the coast between Cherbourg and here is well known to produce quite strong seabreezes.
Morn.	Occ.	All	SW-S/NE (3)	W-NW	M 48	
Aft.	Few	NW (nw/se)	W-SW/NE (12)	W/E-NE (1)	A 51	
Eve.	Few	NE/SW (e)	NW-SW/NE (7)	NE (1)	M 53	
SUMMER						
Morn.	Occ.	All (e-se)	W-SW (1)	—	J 57	
Aft.	Few	SW-W/NE (se)	NW-SW (4)	—	J 62	
Eve.	Few	SW-N (s-ne)	W-SW (1)	—	A 63	
AUTUMN						
Morn.	Occ.	All	NW-SW (4)	—	S 61	
Aft.	Occ.	All	NW-S/NE (6)	W	O 58	
Eve.	Occ.	All	W-S (4)	W-SW (1)	N 54	

French Biscay Coast – North: Brest to Sables d'Oleron (*see Map 9*)

GENERAL FEATURES

Here is a long highly indented coast where all kinds of conditions may be found. The coast starts off facing almost south and ends up facing west, and there are occasional offshore islands.

MAJOR WINDS

It is difficult to find reliable wind information for this coast but we can make inferences about much of it from le Talut on Belle Ile and from Nantes which are twenty miles offshore and inland respectively from the coast.

WINDS (% FREQUENCY) AND SEA TEMPERATURES AT BELLE ILE

	N	NE	E	SE	S	SW	W	NW	Calm	Sea temperatures (°F)		Remarks
SPRING												In the mornings the wind blows mainly off the land but despite being so far from the mainland Belle Ile picks up winds from Biscay with the day in all seasons but particularly in summer. The most likely strong wind directions are from between NW and SW with some northerly ones in summer and autumn plus the onshore feed that is such a summer feature of this and other related coasts.
Morn.	9	18	9	7	5	9	8	8	7	M	51	
Aft.	6	9	8	9	8	9	12	10	4	A	52	
Eve.					[No data]					M	55	
SUMMER												
Morn.	8	16	10	2	5	11	13	15	8	J	60	
Aft.	3	6	7	9	7	15	24	9	4	J	63	
Eve.					[No data]					A	64	
AUTUMN												
Morn.	11	17	9	5	5	7	9	10	6	S	64	
Aft.	5	11	9	7	5	8	13	13	4	O	58	
Eve.					[No data]					N	55	

WINDS AND SEA TEMPERATURES AT NANTES

	Calm	Force 1-4	Force 5-6	Force 7+	Sea temperatures (°F)		Remarks
SPRING							If you sail on waters inland from the coast then Nantes shows the trends. Mornings are calm very often but the wind has picked up by lunchtime and it blows as a seabreeze up the river. In summer, by evening, it is the odd day that does not have a wind from the sea. This is where the stronger winds come from but there are very few above Force 5-6.
Morn.	Many	All	NW/SW (1)	—	M		
Aft.	Few	All	SW-N (1)	—	A	N/A	
Eve.	Occ.	W (se)	SW (1)	—	M		
SUMMER							
Morn.	Many	All	—	—	J		
Aft.	Few	W-SW (se)	W-SW (2)	—	J	N/A	
Eve.	Few	W (e-se)	W-SW (1)	—	A		
AUTUMN							
Morn.	Often	All	SW (1)	—	S		
Aft.	Occ.	W-SW	W (2)	—	O	N/A	
Eve.	Occ.	NE (se)	W-S (1)	—	N		

French Biscay Coast – South: Sables d'Oleron to Spanish Border (see Map 9)

GENERAL FEATURES

Beyond the large mouth of the Gironde we enter the realm of the 'Great Beach', the immensely long coast of sand dunes that is called Les Landes. There are no places of any size on this coast but we can sample the winds at Cazaux on one of the several étangs that lie 4–5 miles inland from the main sea coast.

MAJOR WINDS

The wind regime becomes a very light one in the middle reaches of this coast but at the northern end the coast is very fragmented and there will be a wide range of conditions around Ile d'Oleron etc. As we reach the Spanish border the Pyrenees begin to assert their influence and there are mountain winds to be found.

NOTE

The sea temperatures given for Cazaux are for the open coast of Les Landes.

WINDS (% FREQUENCY) AND SEA TEMPERATURES AT CAZAUX

	N	NE	E	SE	S	SW	W	NW	Calm	Sea temperatures (°F)		Remarks
SPRING												There are very few strong winds to be had here, in fact most of the percentage frequencies given do not include any Force 4–5 winds. The vast numbers of calms which still persist into the middle of the day show that the étangs are not the places for interesting sailing.
Morn.	6	4	1	2	6	6	9	4	60	M	54	
Aft.	7	5	4	3	5	11	19	16	25	A	55	
Eve.					[No data]					M	57	
SUMMER												
Morn.	3	3	3	2	3	3	10	4	67	J	62	
Aft.	5	3	5	4	4	13	28	16	21	J	64	
Eve.					[No data]					A	66	
AUTUMN												
Morn.	4	2	2	2	7	5	9	2	67	S	64	
Aft.	11	6	8	4	9	11	17	8	25	O	60	
Eve.					[No data]					N	53	

WINDS AND SEA TEMPERATURES AT BIARRITZ (PTE DE SOCOA)

	Calm	Force 1–4	Force 5–6	Force 7+	Sea temperatures (°F)		Remarks
SPRING							Biarritz is becoming Mediterranean in its very strong sea-breeze effect which is at its strongest in summer. However, it also shows what happens at a place where the mountains are not far away – in this case to the south. Morning winds are predominantly off the mountains and are sometimes strong, but by midday those directions see no winds that are worth talking about while the sea wind blows in almost universally and fresh to strong sometimes.
Morn.	Occ.	S-SW (n)	S-SE/W-NW (7)	S-SW (2)	M	55	
Aft.	Few	NW (e-s)	W-S (3)	S/NW (1)	A	56	
Eve.	Occ.	NW-N (e-se) (7)	All (ne-se) (7)	W-NW (2)	M	57	
SUMMER							
Morn.	Occ.	S-SW (n-ne)	W-S (4)	SW-W (1)	J	63	
Aft.	Few	W-NW (s-se)	W-S (7)	—	J	65	
Eve.	Occ.	W-NW (sw-e)	W-NW (6)	W (1)	A	67	
AUTUMN							
Morn.	Occ.	S-SE (n-ne)	W-S (8)	S (1)	S	65	
Aft.	Few	NW-N (se)	W-S (8)	W	O	60	
Eve.	Occ.	All	All (ne-se) (5)	NW (1)	N	55	

Iberia: North Coast (*see Map 9*)

GENERAL FEATURES

The high ground stands so close along the sea on this coast that only occasionally are there small coastal plains.

MAJOR WINDS

Winds at sea off this coast show a westerly or easterly trend if they are moderate to fresh, but the lighter winds are hauled on-shore by the hot sierras even from quite far out. The fresh to strong winds are also parallel to the coast and may get up to gale force but the frequencies are low throughout the seasons.

WINDS AND SEA TEMPERATURES AT SANTANDER

	Calm	Force 1–4	Force 5–6	Force 7+	Sea temperatures (°F)	Remarks
SPRING						Although it is sheltered this place shows what happens at a sheltered place that looks out to sea and inland to high mountains. Except in summer the mountain wind blows from S and may well become fresh to strong – even gale. Otherwise the winds are along the coast mainly from W. or sometimes E. In the middle of the day, and into the evening, the sea wind is brought in from NW only to be ousted by the mountain wind in the evening.
Morn.	Mainly	S (nw–ne)	S/NW (4)	S (1)	M 55	
Aft.	No data	No data	No data	No data	A 56	
Eve.	Many	E–NE (sw/se)	NW–W/S (4)	NW	M 58	
SUMMER						
Morn.	Mainly	S (ne–nw)	–	N–W (1)	J 62	
Aft.	No data	No data	No data	No data	J 65	
Eve.	Often	NW (s–se)	W–NW (1)	NW	A 65	
AUTUMN						
Morn.	Often	S/NW (se–n)	NW–S (6)	W/S (1)	S 65	
Aft.	No data	No data	No data	No data	O 60	
Eve.	Often	All (n)	W–NW/S (7)	W/S	N 56	

WINDS (% FREQUENCY) AND SEA TEMPERATURES AT LA CORUÑA

	N	NE	E	SE	S	SW	W	NW	Calm	Sea temperatures (°F)	Remarks
SPRING											La Coruña is on the Ría de la Betanzos – one of the larger of the many indentations on the extreme northwest of Iberia. The major morning wind directions in spring are mainly off the land but swing more westerly in summer. They are replaced by winds off the sea from N or NW. The trend continues on into autumn. There is nearly always wind to be found.
Morn.	9	13	4	13	23	20	8	6	5	M 55	
Aft.	26	11	1	3	9	13	15	19	2	A 57	
Eve.				[No data]						M 60	
SUMMER											
Morn.	13	12	2	7	17	22	10	12	6	J 62	
Aft.	32	7	0	1	3	10	19	29	1	J 66	
Eve.				[No data]						A 66	
AUTUMN											
Morn.	9	7	2	19	28	16	8	8	2	S 65	
Aft.	20	13	1	6	12	15	17	16	3	O 61	
Eve.				[No data]						N 58	

Atlantic Coast of Iberia: Cape Finisterre to Lisbon (see Map 10)

GENERAL FEATURES

From C. Finisterre down to Porto the sierras stand very close to the sea. Then as far as C. Carvoeiro the mountains pull back from the sea until the Sa. do Aire comes down to C. Raso and shelters Lisbon and its harbour which is the estuary of the R. Tejo.

MAJOR WINDS

It is off this coast that the Portuguese trade winds blow. The winds blow predominantly from north through the seasons with the northerlies making over half the winds that blow in summer and almost as many in spring. The trend falters in autumn. On the coast the mountain winds by night and the sea winds by day form the familiar pattern.

WINDS (% FREQUENCY) AND SEA TEMPERATURES AT PORTO

	N	NE	E	SE	S	SW	W	NW	Calm	Sea temperatures (°F)	Remarks
SPRING											At Porto, and very likely other places on this coast, the wind swings from mainly NE or E (mountain wind) to NW or W (seabreeze) at all seasons, but the shift is greatest in summer when there are the greatest number of early morning calms. Only in autumn do we see the effect of the 'trades' when northerlies get up with the day.
Morn.	6	20	21	8	11	8	11	11	4	M 56	
Aft.	8	1	6	2	8	13	25	35	0	A 58	
Eve.					[No data]					M 61	
SUMMER											
Morn.	11	14	13	5	10	10	10	12	15	J 63	
Aft.	11	1	1	0	2	8	27	48	0	J 66	
Eve.					[No data]					A 67	
AUTUMN											
Morn.	7	23	24	8	13	5	3	6	12	S 65	
Aft.	23	10	2	3	11	20	13	18	1	O 64	
Eve.					[No data]					N 60	

WINDS AND SEA TEMPERATURES AT LISBON

	Calm	Force 1-4	Force 5-6	Force 7+	Sea temperatures (°F)	Remarks
SPRING						The north wind certainly blows at Lisbon and on summer mornings over half the winds are from N. By afternoon this northerly trend has increased so that, together with the winds off the sea, no other winds amount to anything. The stronger winds in summer all come from N or NW but may come from anywhere between N and S through W on spring and autumn afternoons.
Morn.	Few	N-NE (sw)	N-NE/SW-S (3)	—	M 57	
Aft.	Few	N/SW (se)	All (ne-se) (6)	—	A 59	
Eve.	No data	No data	No data	No data	M 62	
SUMMER						
Morn.	Few	N (se)	N-NW (1)	—	J 65	
Aft.	Few	N (e-s)	N-NW (4)	—	J 66	
Eve.	No data	No data	No data	No data	A 68	
AUTUMN						
Morn.	Few	NE-N (se)	N-NW/SW (2)	—	S 66	
Aft.	Few	N/SW (se)	All (ne-se) (3)	—	O 65	
Eve.	No data	No data	No data	No data	N 62	

Southwestern Coasts of Iberia: Lisbon to Gibraltar (see Map 10)

GENERAL FEATURES

From Lisbon southwards to C. de Sines the high ground is well inland. Then the sierras stretch down into the southwest tip of Portugal to where it turns the corner at C. de São Vicente. Then up to the Gulf of Cadiz there is a moderate coastal plain, followed by the low coast of Andalucia that stretches down southeastwards to the Strait of Gibraltar.

MAJOR WINDS

Off the west-facing coast the Portuguese trades still blow and these northerlies keep a grip on the wind direction along the coast except where mountain winds by night and seabreezes by day override them.

WINDS AND SEA TEMPERATURES AT FARO

	Calm	Force 1-4	Force 5-6	Force 7+	Sea temperatures (°F)	Remarks
SPRING						Faro is on the coastal plain of the Algarve where it projects out to C. de Santa Maria. It is representative of the coastal plain here which is backed by the sierras until we get to the Spanish border. There is a great trend to easterly winds here except in high summer when the sea-breeze takes over the day. Other than that the winds blow from W (or E) when they are fresh to strong – which is not often.
Morn.	Often	All	NW-SW/E (3)	E-SE	M 59	
Aft.	Occ.	E(ne-n)	S-SW (2)	—	A 62	
Eve.	Occ.	SW (n-ne)	NW-S (8)	W-SW (1)	M 64	
SUMMER						
Morn.	Many	E-S (ne)	E-SE/W-NW (1)	—	J 67	
Aft.	Occ.	W-SW/E (ne)	—	—	J 69	
Eve.	Occ.	SW-SE (n-ne)	W-SW/E (4)	W (1)	A 71	
AUTUMN						
Morn.	Many	E (n)	NW-S/E-NE (2)	—	S 70	
Aft.	Occ.	E (se)	—	—	O 68	
Eve.	Occ.	SW-E (ne)	NW-S/E (2)	—	N 64	

WINDS (% FREQUENCY) AND SEA TEMPERATURES AT SAN FERNANDO

	N	NE	E	SE	S	SW	W	NW	Calm	Sea temperatures (°F)	Remarks
SPRING											San Fernando is just south of Cadiz and on the coast. The coastal plain is wide and all the lighter morning winds from the land tend to swing in off the sea from W or SW by afternoon in summer and autumn but not so much in spring.
Morn.	7	8	21	16	5	7	13	17	7	M	
Aft.	3	2	14	11	7	14	30	16	0	A N/A	
Eve.				[No data]						M	
SUMMER											
Morn.	7	4	22	17	13	7	12	14	6	J	
Aft.	0	0	16	9	5	17	41	12	0	J N/A	
Eve.				[No data]						A	
AUTUMN											
Morn.	8	11	26	19	6	4	7	10	11	S	
Aft.	5	2	14	11	10	13	29	16	1	O N/A	
Eve.				[No data]						N	

Madeira and the Canary Islands

GENERAL FEATURES

These two groups of islands lie in semi-tropical waters off the coast of Morocco. They are not difficult to get to by air and so have become places for sailing on an all-the-year-round basis. There are long periods of settled weather interspersed with less settled and at times stormy weather when arms of the Atlantic depressions sweep across the area. However, the seas are warm and the general climate mild.

MAJOR WINDS

The islands are in the compass of the northeast trade winds and so up to 40 per cent of the winds come from NE in winter and up to 60 per cent in summer. Gales interrupt this flow, occurring for about six hours in a week's stay on average in January, but only for about an hour in any representative summer week.

NOTES

The very low frequencies of NE winds at Funchal is a local effect. Madeira lies in waters where, away from the coasts, three quarters of the winds that blow are from NE in summer and over a third are from NE in winter.

WINDS (% FREQUENCY) AND SEA TEMPERATURES AT FUNCHAL (MADEIRA)

	N	NE	E	SE	S	SW	W	NW	Calm	Sea temperatures (°F)		Remarks
SPRING												Madeira lies just outside the throw of the Trades and so as Funchal itself is sheltered from north we find very few northerlies.
Morn.	3	2	5	16	20	18	9	2	25	M	62	
Aft.	2	2	4	18	28	28	12	2	6	A	64	
Eve.					[No data]					M	65	
SUMMER												The major wind directions are S and SW and these pick up with the day in all seasons. There are always going to be marked variations on volcanic islands like this.
Morn.	1	1	1	14	31	27	2	0	22	J	68	
Aft.	1	1	1	9	40	40	4	0	5	J	70	
Eve.					[No data]					A	73	
AUTUMN												
Morn.	6	5	5	12	15	13	6	2	36	S	73	
Aft.	3	3	5	15	28	24	10	2	8	O	72	
Eve.					[No data]					N	68	

WINDS (% FREQUENCY) AND SEA TEMPERATURES AT SANTA CRUZ DE TENERIFFE

	N	NE	E	SE	S	SW	W	NW	Calm	Sea temperatures (°F)		Remarks
SPRING												The Canaries are well in the Trades and exhibit the behaviour of Trades. The wind blows from other directions overnight but picks up from NE with the day.
Morn.	15	9	2	1	2	4	20	33	14	M	64	
Aft.	12	21	20	6	9	8	4	21	0	A	65	
Eve.					[No data]					M	67	
SUMMER												We see that the morning direction that is favoured is NW and in summer NW and calm amount to over half the morning winds,
Morn.	15	13	2	1	3	5	10	22	29	J	70	
Aft.	14	27	30	5	6	4	2	10	3	J	71	
Eve.					[No data]					A	72	
AUTUMN												but by midday the same number blow from NE or E.
Morn.	18	12	4	1	1	2	22	24	15	S	72	
Aft.	14	24	24	8	9	4	1	13	1	O	72	
Eve.					[No data]					N	71	

Mediterranean South Coast of Spain: Gibraltar to Cabo de Gata (see Map 11)

GENERAL FEATURES

Beyond the curiosity of the Rock of Gibraltar the high sierras come close to the sea all the way along the Costa del Sol. In the major gaps lie the major towns of Málaga and Almería before the coast turns northeastward and the Mediterranean widens. The waterway facing the Costa del Sol is the Alborán Channel with Morocco on the opposite shore.

MAJOR WINDS

Winds blow through the narrow Strait of Gibraltar either from W or E and this is also the regime at sea in the Alborán Channel. The east wind is the Levanter and the west wind is the Vendeval. The form of scirroco called Chili blows across these waters from S.

WINDS AND SEA TEMPERATURES AT MÁLAGA

○ Jn-A (17) ● N-Mr (5)	Calm	Force 1-4	Force 5-6	Force 7+	Sea temperatures (°F)	Remarks
SPRING						Tucked away in a gap between two sierras Málaga is so well sheltered that no strong to gale winds are reported. Down on the coasts of the Costa del Sol it will blow harder but the Levanter and Vendeval do not reach here. Mornings are calm or have wind from the valley to the northwest. Days are dominated by gentle seabreeze but by early evening it is back to calm and mountain wind.
Morn.	Many	NW (s-se)	NW only (1)	—	M 58	
Aft.	Occ.	SE-SW (ne)	NW-SW (4)	—	A 60	
Eve.	Many	NW/SE (n)	NW only (1)	—	M 62	
SUMMER						
Morn.	Many	NW (s/e)	—	—	J 65	
Aft.	Occ.	S-SE (n-e)	SE-E (1)	—	J 72	
Eve.	Often	NW (n-ne)	—	—	A 72	
AUTUMN						
Morn.	Many	NW (s-se)	NE only (1)	—	S 70	
Aft.	Occ.	SE-S (n-ne)	NW-S (1)	—	O 66	
Eve.	Many	NW/SE	NW only (1)	—	N 68	

WINDS AND SEA TEMPERATURES AT ALMERÍA

○ Jy-A (16) ● J-Mr (4)	Calm	Force 1-4	Force 5-6	Force 7+	Sea temperatures (°F)	Remarks
SPRING						Almería is as windy a place as Málaga is quiet. Here we see the trend to winds from westerly or easterly points plus a sierra wind in the mornings and a seabreeze by day. Almería's winds can be taken to represent the coast where it is not protected by headlands and bays while sheltered places will be more like Málaga.
Morn.	Many	NE-N	N-NE/N-SW (7)	SW (1)	M 58	
Aft.	Few	SW-S (nw-e)	W-S-E (23)	W-SW/E (10)	A 60	
Eve.	Occ.	SW-S (nw-n)	W-SW/E (20)	W-SW (7)	M 63	
SUMMER						
Morn.	Many	NE (nw)	S only (5)	W-SW (1)	J 66	
Aft.	Few	SW-S (nw-e)	SW/SE-E (20)	W-SW (4)	J 70	
Eve.	Few	SW-S (nw-ne)	All (nw-n) (20)	W-SW/E (6)	A 75	
AUTUMN						
Morn.	Many	NE-N (se)	W-SW/N (5)	W-SW (1)	S 73	
Aft.	Few	S-SW (nw-n)	All (nw-n) (20)	W-SW (6)	O 70	
Eve.	Occ.	SW (nw)	W-SW/E (14)	W-SW (5)	N 69	

Spanish Mediterranean Coast: Cabo de Gata to Golfo de Valencia (see Map 11)

GENERAL FEATURES

The high ground is never far from the sea on this coast but there are certainly more stretches of coastal plain than on the Sierra Nevada coast, and between Cartagena and Alicante as well as round Valencia itself the coastal plains are moderately wide. Also on the northern portion of this coast the sierras are not as high as further south.

MAJOR WINDS

The NE wind called the Levante blows onto this coast while the southerly wind from the desert is called the Leveche. Levante brings squalls and accompanying bad weather in spring and autumn and its origin may have been bora gales in the Adriatic. Otherwise the regime is mountain wind by night and seabreeze by day.

WINDS AND SEA TEMPERATURES AT ALICANTE

○ Jn-A (20) ● N-D (5)	Calm	Force 1-4	Force 5-6	Force 7+	Sea temperatures (°F)	Remarks
SPRING						Alicante lies on a narrow coastal strip with the high ground orientated southwest to northeast. The effect is to strengthen the NE winds when they occur. However, summer afternoons have an overwhelming preponderance of SE seabreezes that can get up to strong to gale. The strong wind has died down by evening, however. There are many morning calms as the seabreeze reverses the night wind.
Mom.	Many	N-NW (se)	W-NE (4)	NE-E (1)	M 57	
Aft.	Few	E-S (n-ne)	S-NE/W (5)	SE-N/W (5)	A 59	
Eve.	Occ.	E-SE (sw)	E-NE/W-NW (4)	E/W-NW (1)	M 63	
SUMMER						
Mom.	Many	N-NE	NE/NW (3)	—	J 69	
Aft.	Few	E-S only	S-NE (23)	SE-NE (4)	J 75	
Eve.	Occ.	E-SE (sw)	E-NE (6)	E (1)	A 77	
AUTUMN						
Mom.	Many	NW-N (s-e)	N-W (4)	NW/NE (1)	S 75	
Aft.	Occ.	SE (nw-n/s)	All (15)	NE-E/W-SW (2)	O 70	
Eve.	Often	All	NE-E/NW (4)	—	N 64	

WINDS AND SEA TEMPERATURES AT VALENCIA

○ Jy-A (16) ● N-F (6)	Calm	Force 1-4	Force 5-6	Force 7+	Sea temperatures (°F)	Remarks
SPRING						The mornings are often calm, with light mountain wind down the valley of the R. Turia at other times. No data exists for afternoons but we can infer a very strong seabreeze shift to between NE and SE in spring and summer which we see still blows in the evening. The strongest winds experienced are NE in autumn and will be the Levante, but strong winds are much less in evidence here than further south.
Mom.	Many	NW-SW (s-e)	W-SW (1)	—	M 54	
Aft.	No data	No data	No data	No data	A 55	
Eve.	Occ.	SE-NE (nw)	W-NW (1)	W (2)	M 61	
SUMMER						
Mom.	Mainly	W-NE (s-e)	SE (1)	W-NW (1)	J 69	
Aft.	No data	No data	No data	No data	J 75	
Eve.	Many	NE-SE (w-nw)	NE/SE (1)	—	A 76	
AUTUMN						
Mom.	Many	W-NW (s-ne)	W-NW (1)	NE (1)	S 71	
Aft.	No data	No data	No data	No data	O 68	
Eve.	Many	All	W/NE (2)	—	N 60	

The Balearics (see Map 11)

GENERAL FEATURES

Mallorca is large enough to produce a strong seabreeze effect. Its highest point is some 4,000 ft above the sea. Ibiza is also high for its size while the island of intermediate size, Menorca, is lower. With coasts facing all directions on-shore, side-shore or off-shore conditions may be found but these sunlit islands can induce seabreezes of some magnitude.

MAJOR WINDS

The sea area in which the Balearics stand shows trends to having most winds from either W–SW or E–NE and the gales certainly come from these directions.

WINDS (% FREQUENCY) AND SEA TEMPERATURES AT PALMA DE MALLORCA

○ J–A (18) ● N–J (6)

	N	NE	E	SE	S	SW	W	NW	Calm	Sea temperatures (°F)	Remarks
SPRING											These figures show how strong the seabreeze effect is on the southern side of Mallorca at all seasons, and particularly in summer when two-thirds of the winds are from SW. However, the wind drains off the land during the night even though Mallorca is not a large island.
Morn.	34	21	7	1	6	14	8	8	0	M 57	
Aft.	11	12	7	1	9	47	9	4	0	A 58	
Eve.					[No data]					M 62	
SUMMER											
Morn.	26	27	11	2	8	18	5	3	0	J 69	
Aft.	5	5	5	1	8	67	5	2	0	J 73	
Eve.					[No data]					A 76	
AUTUMN											
Morn.	47	22	5	1	2	8	8	7	0	S 75	
Aft.	18	13	7	2	7	37	11	6	0	O 69	
Eve.					[No data]					N 65	

WINDS AND SEA TEMPERATURES AT PUERTO DE MAHÓN (MENORCA)

○ J–A (20) ● N–F (6)

	Calm	Force 1–4	Force 5–6	Force 7+	Sea temperatures (°F)	Remarks
SPRING						Mahón is on the eastern side of Menorca but this does not account for the trend there is to have strong northerly winds throughout the year. This wind is the Tramontana which is the outflow from the mountains of the French and Italian coasts. Mahón is well sheltered and so it must be remembered that wherever you sail on a small island the wind will tend to blow directly on-shore by day but will be bent by the local terrain.
Morn.	Mainly	All	N/SW (7)	N (2)	M 57	
Aft.	Few	S (w)	All (w/e) (8)	NW–NE (2)	A 58	
Eve.	Occ.	All	All (w/e) (7)	W–NW (1)	M 62	
SUMMER						
Morn.	Mainly	All	N–NE/SW–S (3)	N (2)	J 69	
Aft.	Few	NE/S (w)	NW–NE/SW–S (6)	N	J 73	
Eve.	Occ.	S/N–NE (w)	N–NW/SW–W (4)	N–NE	A 76	
AUTUMN						
Morn.	Mainly	All	N–NW/SE (5)	N (1)	S 75	
Aft.	Few	All	N–NE/SE (7)	N (2)	O 69	
Eve.	Often	All	N/E–SE/W (6)	N (1)	N 65	

Valencia to Perpignan (see Map 12)

GENERAL FEATURES

The coastline is one great gentle curve up to and beyond Barcelona, where the Costa Brava starts. All along the coast the mountains are not far from the sea and the only feature to break up the smoothness of the curve is the silt of the estuary of the R. Ebro at C. Tortosa. Then at C. de San Sebastian the coast abruptly turns north eventually to merge into the coastal flatlands of the westerward extension of the Camargues.

MAJOR WINDS

Here, as we go further north into the Gulf of Lion, we are entering mistral country. The mistral-type mountain wind has many names along this coast. It is the Cierzo in the Ebro valley, the Cers in the Aude valley near Perpignan, the Mestral in Catalonia, etc. (See next section.)

WINDS AND SEA TEMPERATURES AT BARCELONA

○ Jy-A (11) ● M-My/O-D (8)	Calm	Force 1-4	Force 5-6	Force 7+	Sea temperatures (°F)	Remarks
SPRING						The mountain slope wind at Barcelona is the maestral and blows strongest from NW. The NE strong winds are levante gales which are extensions of the mistral when it blows into the Gulf of Lion. On summer days the mornings are all mountain wind and no winds from the sea. By afternoon it is all winds from the sea and no winds from the land.
Morn.	Many	N-W (se)	N-NE (2)	NE-E (2)	M 55	
Aft.	Occ.	SW-S	SW-NW/E-NE (5)	NW/SE (1)	A 57	
Eve.	Many	N-NW (s-se)	SW-W/E-NE (5)	SW/NE (1)	M 60	
SUMMER						
Morn.	Many	N (s-se)	W/E (1)	W/N (1)	J 67	
Aft.	Occ.	SW-SE (w-ne)	W-SE (2)	S-SE (1)	J 72	
Eve.	Occ.	SW-E (nw-n)	W-SW/E (2)	SW (1)	A 74	
AUTUMN						
Morn.	Many	N-NW (s-se)	W-N (2)	NW-N (1)	S 72	
Aft.	Occ.	SW-E	NW-N (1)	NW/SE (1)	O 67	
Eve.	Many	W-SW	W/N/SE (2)	—	N 61	

WINDS AND SEA TEMPERATURES AT PERPIGNAN

○ Jy-A (11) ● M-My (14)	Calm	Force 1-4	Force 5-6	Force 7+	Sea temperatures (°F)	Remarks
SPRING						Because it is some miles in from the main sea coast and the nearest high ground is to the northwest, Perpignan does not show a strong seabreeze regime. Down on the coast there will be more sea winds than indicated here, but even so the trend always to have fresh or more off-shore winds will make this coast one where seabreezes are not to be relied on. Winds from the SE follow the trend shown at Cap Béar to the southeast. At the latter, winds of all seasons are mainly NW or, slightly less often, SE. Gales tend to be from NW-N.
Morn.	Many	NW-SW only	W-NW (12)	W-NW (1)	M 54	
Aft.	Occ.	E-SE (s-w)	W-NW (20)	W-NW (1)	A 55	
Eve.	Many	All (sw)	W-NW/S-SE (15)	W-NW/SE (1)	M 59	
SUMMER						
Morn.	Many	NW-W (s-ne)	W-N (10)	W-NW (1)	J 66	
Aft.	Occ.	All (sw-s)	W-N (13)	W-SW (1)	J 70	
Eve.	Occ.	All (sw-s)	W-NW (14)	SW (1)	A 70	
AUTUMN						
Morn.	Mainly	NW-W (sw-ne)	W-N (7)	NW (1)	S 68	
Aft.	Many	All (s-sw)	W-NW/S-SE (15)	W-NW (1)	O 63	
Eve.	Many	All (sw-s/ne)	W-NW/SE (10)	—	N 59	

Gulf of Lion: Perpignan to Marseille
(see Map 12)

GENERAL FEATURES

Beyond Perpignan, apart from near C. Leucate, the mountains draw back and we enter a low coast with the lagoons of the Camargues that ends in the Rhône Valley.

MAJOR WINDS

This is the coast of the mistral proper. The mistral is a mountain-gap wind that comes when the isobars are for winds from the northern side of the mountains. Cool air then builds up against the Massif Centrale and the Alps and eventually bursts through the gaps. The major gaps are those created by the rivers Rhône and Garonne. Strength is the major feature of the mistral which often blows at gale force under clear skies. The coast considered here is the most exposed, while further on towards the Gulf of Genoa there is much shelter from the worst effects. The mistral is also a very gusty wind which can capsize dinghies and make boardsailing very difficult if not impossible for most people. The table above opposite shows that March is the worst month for the mistral, but even in summer it has near gale strength on an average four days a month. Average numbers of days in each month with a mistral of Force 6 or above between Perpignan and Marseille are also shown opposite.

Except in October and November there is widespread mistral affecting most of the coasts on an average of two days a month. The table is for mistral somewhere, and sometimes the high speed corridor may be relatively narrow. Some parts are more prone than others and it is best to enquire locally how likely it is that the wind blows there.

THE MISTRAL-SEABREEZE EFFECT

Because the mistral opposes the seabreeze and the latter's force can be quite strong, when the lower mistral wind speeds occur in the mornings the seabreeze effect slows the wind during the middle of the day and thus creates a double-humped wind speed regime. The highest speed may be reached at 1000 in summer and 1200 in winter. The wind then goes down during the succeeding hours to rise again in the evening as the seabreeze's influence wanes.

	Jan	Feb	Mar	Apr	May	Jun	Jul	Aug	Sep	Oct	Nov	Dec
Force 6	10	9	13	11	8	9	9	7	5	5	7	10
Force 7	8	6	10	9	6	4	4	3	2	2	3	7
Force 8	6	6	9	5	4	2	2	2	2	0	0	5

WINDS (DAYLIGHT HOURS) AND SEA TEMPERATURES ON THE CAMARGUES COAST (CAP DE SÈTE)

○ Jy-A (18) ● N-D/Mr (15)	Calm	Force 1-4	Force 5-6	Force 7+	Sea temperatures (°F)	Remarks
SPRING	Few	NW but all	NW (20) SE (5)	NW/E-SE (4)	M 54 / A 55 / M 60	The major pattern will be the familiar one of morning NW wind that is reduced in speed and may often be reversed into a seabreeze.
SUMMER	Occ.	NW but all	NW (10)	NW (2)	J 66 / J 70 / A 71	
AUTUMN	Occ.	NW but all	NW (10) SE (5)	NW/SE (4)	S 70 / O 66 / N 61	

WINDS (DAYLIGHT HOURS) AND SEA TEMPERATURES IN THE MARSEILLE AREA (CAP CROISETTE)

○ Jy-A (18) ● N-D/Mr (15)	Calm	Force 1-4	Force 5-6	Force 7+	Sea temperatures (°F)	Remarks
SPRING	Occ.	NW-W/E-SE (ne)	NW (15)	W-NW/E (5)	M 54 / A 55 / M 60	Cap Croisette is more representative than Marseille for the latter's winds are recorded at the air base of Marignone some 15 miles to the northeast. The coast grows high here and so the winds tend to canalise one way or the other along the coast. Even so the NW wind beats all others for strength.
SUMMER	Occ.	NW-W/E-SE (ne/s)	NW (10)	NW (1)	J 66 / J 70 / A 71	
AUTUMN	Occ.	NW/E-SE (ne/s-se)	NW (10) E-SE (10)	NW/E-SE (4)	S 70 / O 66 / N 61	

Côte d'Azur and the Gulf of Genoa

(see Map 12)

GENERAL FEATURES

The Alpes de Provence, Alpi Maritime and Appino Ligure rise to great heights inland from this coast. The mountains dip into the sea for long stretches with only occasional gaps. The beaches are often rocky and a constant watch should be kept on the possibility of falling winds overtaking an otherwise light wind regime.

MAJOR WINDS

The mistral continues to blow along this coast. Offshore it turns more easterly and becomes the Libeccio, while in the Gulf of Genoa it is the Tramontana. As mentioned above this can be a dangerous coast to sail off the beach as sudden intense squalls may appear over the cliffs or other coastal high land.

NOTES

Care must be taken to allow for thunderstorms over the rising ground inland. These may lead to downdraught gales appearing at the coast even though the storms may not appear very near. Such winds are cold and blustery. They are off-shore and so potentially dangerous. They seek any gap in the coastal high land or they pour over the cliffs or other bluff coastal land onto the water in what should be their lee.

WINDS AND SEA TEMPERATURES AT NICE

○ Jy-A (20)　　● N-D/Mr (13)

	Calm	Force 1-4	Force 5-6	Force 7+	Sea temperatures (°F)	Remarks
SPRING						Nice is sheltered from the mountain winds but they do occur. However, they are most likely to be light and calms abound night and morning. There is a strong takeover of the afternoons by seabreeze, mainly from SE or S and this continues to blow into the evenings at all seasons. However, expect most seabreeze days to go calm during the evening and then to pick up mountain wind.
Morn.	Many	N (w/s)	NE-E/SW (3)	SW (1)	M 55	
Aft.	Occ.	SE-SW (w-n)	E-SE/SW (10)	SW (2)	A 57	
Eve.	Often	SE-SW (w-n)	W-SW/E (5)	SW (1)	M 61	
SUMMER						
Morn.	Mainly	N (w)	E-SE (1)	—	J 68	
Aft.	Occ.	SE-SW (w-e)	E-SE/W-SW (6)	E-SE/W-SW (1)	J 73	
Eve.	Many	SE-S (w-ne)	SW/SE (4)	SW (1)	A 73	
AUTUMN						
Morn.	Many	N (w-se)	N-SE (1)	—	S 70	
Aft.	Occ.	SE-SW (w-n)	NE-E/SW (4)	SW (1)	O 66	
Eve.	Many	SE (nw)	SW/SE (2)	NE (1)	N 61	

WINDS AND SEA TEMPERATURES AT GENOA

○ Jy-A (16)　　● N-J (10)

	Calm	Force 1-4	Force 5-6	Force 7+	Sea temperatures (°F)	Remarks
SPRING						Genoa is not so sheltered as Nice and there are far fewer calms. Southerly strong winds may well be scirocco which, having travelled so far over the sea, has become moisture-laden and so leads to low cloud and poor visibility. However, once again the most likely daytime wind is a gentle seabreeze that blows on into the evening, although no specific data exist for this time.
Morn.	Often	S-NE (w-nw)	S-SE/N-NE (5)	N (1)	M 55	
Aft.	Occ.	S-SE (nw)	SE/N-NE (4)	N (1)	A 57	
Eve.	No data	No data	No data	No data	M 62	
SUMMER						
Morn.	Occ.	SE-S (w-nw)	S-SE/N-NE (2)	—	J 69	
Aft.	Few.	SE-SW (nw/ne)	S-SE/N (2)	—	J 73	
Eve.	No data	No data	No data	No data	A 74	
AUTUMN						
Morn.	Occ.	N-NE (w-sw)	N-NE/S (10)	N-NE (1)	S 71	
Aft.	Occ.	SE-S/N (w)	N-NE/S-SE (8)	W-NE (1)	O 68	
Eve.	No data	No data	No data	No data	N 62	

Corsica and Sardinia (see Map 12)

GENERAL FEATURES

These two high islands have very few coastal plains. They sit fully in the Mediterranean sun and so will exhibit thermal winds wherever there is shelter. However, they also lie in the path of the Libeccio and to the south of the Gulf of Genoa, which is well known as a centre where Mediterranean-bred depressions are born.

MAJOR WINDS

Here we see the effects of the mountain winds that pour off the Pyrenees, the Monts Corbières, the Massif Centrale and the French Alps. These feed one of the sources of the summer 'monsoon' that eventually finds its journey's end in North Africa. However, the Adriatic bora also feeds across Italy and so out over the islands on its way to becoming the Levante and Levanter of the Spanish coasts.

WINDS AND SEA TEMPERATURES AT CAP CORSE

○ Jy-A (18) ● N-D/Mr (14)

	Calm	Force 1-4	Force 5-6	Force 7+	Sea temperatures (°F)	Remarks
SPRING						
Mom.	Occ.	W-SW/E-SE (n/s)	NW-SW/NE-SE (14)	NW-SW/SE (5)	M 56	Cap Corse is on the northernmost extremity of Corsica and shows a remarkable tendency to have westerly winds that increase in frequency through the afternoon and continue into the evening. Thus they must be breeze being pulled from the Italian coast which lies over 50 miles to the east. This shows how powerful the seabreeze effect is in the Mediterranean. The other main direction is NE.
Aft.	Occ.	W (s)	W/NE-SE (14)	W-SW/SE (4)	A 57	
Eve.	Occ.	W (s)	NW-SW (14)	NW-SW (5)	M 62	
SUMMER						
Mom.	Occ.	W-SW (n/s)	W-SW/NE/SE (10)	NW-SW/NE-E (4)	J 70	
Aft.	Occ.	W (s)	NW-SW/NE-SE (10)	W-SW/SE (5)	J 73	
Eve.	Occ.	W (s/n)	NW-SW/SE (9)	NW-SW (5)	A 75	
AUTUMN						
Mom.	Occ.	All (n)	All (12)	NW-S (5)	S 72	
Aft.	Occ.	W (s)	NW-SW/NE-SE (12)	NW-SW (5)	O 67	
Eve.	Occ.	W (s)	All (10)	NW-SW (6)	N 62	

WINDS AND SEA TEMPERATURES AT CAP PERTUSATO

○ Jy-A (19) ● N-J/Mr (14)

	Calm	Force 1-4	Force 5-6	Force 7+	Sea temperatures (°F)	Remarks
SPRING						
Mom.	Few	W (nw-n/s-se)	NW-SW/NE-SE (16)	W-NW/NE (5)	M 55	Cap Pertusato lies on the southern extremity of Corsica and shows the strong wind regime in the Strait of Bonifacio between the islands. The same west-east prevailing winds exist here as at Cap Corse but they are stronger and more frequent. Some of this is funnelling through the Strait but not all of it. These are the winds where the beaches are exposed. Yet where it is sheltered as at Ajaccio hardly any morning is anything other than calm, the afternoon wind is almost all seabreeze or calm and the evening is the same. It all depends on the beach you frequent.
Aft.	Few	W (nw-n/s-se)	NW-SW/NE-E (24)	NW-SW/NE (8)	A 57	
Eve.	Few	W (n/s)	NW-SW/NE-E (20)	NW-SW/ NE-E (7)	M 61	
SUMMER						
Mom.	Occ.	W (nw-n/se-s)	NW-SW/NE-E (11)	NW-SW/E (3)	J 67	
Aft.	Few	W (nw-n/se-s)	NW-SW/NE-E (23)	NW-SW/NE (5)	J 72	
Eve.	Occ.	W (n/s)	NW-SW/NE-E (17)	NW-SW (3)	A 74	
AUTUMN						
Mom.	Occ.	W/NE-E (n/s)	NW-SW/NE-E (14)	SW/NE (5)	S 72	
Aft.	Few	W (nw-n/s-se)	NW-SW/NE-E (22)	NW-SW/E (6)	O 67	
Eve.	Occ.	W/NE (n/s-se)	NW-SW/NE-E (15)	NW-SW/E (5)	N 62	

Italian West Coast: Riviera di Levante to Salerno (*see Map 12*)

GENERAL FEATURES

At first between Genoa and La Spezia the high ground is still very close to the sea. From then on it begins to open out and we enter the realm of the 'great beach' which runs more-or-less from Pisa to Piombino. However, there is still plenty of coastal plain in most places right down to beyond Naples and Salerno after which the coast becomes so rugged and high as to be largely inhospitable.

MAJOR WINDS

The major regional wind is the northerly tramontana, which gets a different name of Greco or Gregale when it blows from NE over the Tyrrhenian Sea. This is the Adriatic bora coming over the Apennines. The wind may be strong, but it is dry and clear on this coast although it can be a violent wind in winter.

WINDS AND SEA TEMPERATURES AT LIVORNO (LEGHORN)

○ Jy-A (17) ● N-F (8)

	Calm	Force 1-4	Force 5-6	Force 7+	Sea temperatures (°F)	Remarks
SPRING						Set on the coast with the valley of the R. Arno stretching inland. Livorno is representative of conditions on the beaches of western Italy. Although we have no data for the afternoon we can expect the situation to be like the early evening (1800) but with more seabreezes, far fewer calms and fewer off-shore winds. Strong wind from SW is libeccio and from S is sometimes scirocco.
Morn.	Many	E-NE (nw-n/sw)	NE-E/W-SW (5)	W-SW (3)	M 55	
Aft.	No data	No data	No data	No data	A 57	
Eve.	Many	NW (se)	W-S-E (4)	W-SW/NE (4)	M 62	
SUMMER						
Morn.	Many	E (nw)	W-SW (4)	W-SW (1)	J 69	
Aft.	No data	No data	No data	No data	J 74	
Eve.	Many	NW-SW (se-ne)	W-S (3)	W-SW (2)	A 74	
AUTUMN						
Morn.	Many	NE-E (nw/s-se)	W-S/NE-E (7)	W-S (3)	S 71	
Aft.	No data	No data	No data	No data	O 67	
Eve.	Many	All (se)	W-S (7)	W-S (5)	N 62	

WINDS AND SEA TEMPERATURES AT NAPLES (CAPODICHINO)

○ Jy-A (23) ● N-D/Mr-Ap (10)

	Calm	Force 1-4	Force 5-6	Force 7+	Sea temperatures (°F)	Remarks
SPRING						The vast number of calms that seem to persist through the day is a quirk of the Bay of Naples. There will be more wind out on the coast. However, southerly seabreezes here are local and will be more westerly out on the coast as appears in the evening statistics. Morning winds are off the Apennines very often and when strong are extensions of the tramontana. Here, because of the shelter, we get strong to gale winds occasionally that do not grow through fresh but suddenly appear.
Morn.	Many	NE/SW (se)	SW-SE/NE (3)	NE-E (1)	M 57	
Aft.	Occ.	S-SW (se-e)	—	W/SE (1)	A 58	
Eve.	Many	W-SW	NW-S/NE-E (5)	—	M 64	
SUMMER						
Morn.	Mainly	NE-N	N-N-S (1)	—	J 71	
Aft.	Occ.	S-SW (e)	—	E (1)	J 74	
Eve.	Many	NW-SW (e-se)	W-NW (1)	—	A 77	
AUTUMN						
Morn.	Many	NE-N	S-E/W (3)	SE-S (1)	S 72	
Aft.	Many	S-SW (se-e)	—	SW-S (1)	O 70	
Eve.	Many	NW-SW (se)	N-W-S (1)	SW (1)	N 65	

West Coast of the 'toe' of Italy: Salerno to Palermo (see Map 13)

GENERAL FEATURES

Beyond Salerno the coast rises straight out of the sea. There are some 'roads' in from the sea where rivers have cut outlets, but on the whole you will find only a few good beaches right down to and including the north coast of Sicily.

MAJOR WINDS

The libeccio drives from NW onto this coast but not strongly. The strong winds come off the inland mountains finding any road they can to the sea or falling over the cliff as sometimes violent squalls, especially if thunderstorms breed over the foothills. If you should sail this coast make sure you know about the possible dangers. Scirocco can be very nasty here.

WINDS AND SEA TEMPERATURES AT PAOLA

○ Jy-A (24) ● D-J (15)	Calm	Force 1-4	Force 5-6	Force 7+	Sea temperatures (°F)	Remarks
SPRING						Paola represents one of those little, very sparse, coastal places where there is some kind of a gap in the continuous run of cliffs. The libeccio shows up in the NW fresh winds and the scirocco in the southerlies. Yet the strength is again off the mountains with the seabreeze fighting the morning winds and not always winning. The NE mornings account for most of the winds at this time.
Mom.	Many	E-NE (sw)	SW-S/NE-E (7)	NE-E (2)	M 57	
Aft.	Some	W-NW (ne)	SW-SE-NE (4)	E-SE (1)	A 61	
Eve.	No data	No data	No data	No data	M 64	
SUMMER						
Mom.	Many	N-E only	NE-E/NW (1)	—	J 71	
Aft.	Occ.	SW-NW (s-se/ne)	NW/SE (3)	—	J 76	
Eve.	No data	No data	No data	No data	A 78	
AUTUMN						
Mom.	Few	N-E (nw-sw)	N-E (6)	NE-N (2)	S 74	
Aft.	Occ.	W-S	NE-SE/NW-W (6)	NE-E (2)	O 70	
Eve.	No data	No data	No data	No data	N 66	

WINDS AND SEA TEMPERATURES AT PALERMO

○ Jy-A (24) ● D-J (15)	Calm	Force 1-4	Force 5-6	Force 7+	Sea temperatures (°F)	Remarks
SPRING						The north coast of Sicily forms the southern flank of a great mountainous bay and at Palermo is found one of the few gaps. The light winds come off the high ground to the southwest and west while the seabreeze blows from NE or E. Gales from W or NW are libeccio, and over the island from S or SE are mainly scirocco. When the latter has a Föhn effect added to its heat and dryness then Palermo can become unbearably hot.
Mom.	Many	W-SW	W-SW/E-NE (2)	W/NE (1)	M 57	
Aft.	Few	NE-E/NW	NW/S-SE (1)	—	A 60	
Eve.	Some	NE-E/NW	N-SW/SE (2)	NW/SE (1)	M 64	
SUMMER						
Mom.	Mainly	All (s)	W-SW (1)	—	J 69	
Aft.	Occ.	NE-E (w-s)	NW (1)	—	J 76	
Eve.	Occ.	NE-E (w-s)	NW/NE (1)	NW (1)	A 79	
AUTUMN						
Mom.	Many	W-SW (se-n)	W-S/NE-E (2)	—	S 76	
Aft.	Many	NE-E (s)	W-SW/NE (1)	—	O 71	
Eve.	Many	All	NW-SW/E (1)	S-SE (1)	N 66	

Sicilian Channel (see Map 13)

GENERAL FEATURES

The Sicilian Channel is where the Western Mediterranean becomes the Eastern Mediterranean. On the northern side we have the high south coast of Sicily. This is more indented than the north coast but still does not provide many beaches. In the middle of the Channel is Malta and Pantelleria and the south side is the coast of Tunisia. This is a high coast around the Gulf of Tunis but the high ground recedes as you go down towards the Gulf of Gabes.

MAJOR WINDS

Like all channels the land directs the winds either up the channel from SE or down it from NW. The NW wind predominates in spring and to a much greater extent in summer, while winds from both directions are equally probable in autumn. This area is close to the desert out of which blows the scirocco.

WINDS AND SEA TEMPERATURES AT MALTA (VALETTA)

○ Jy–A (22) ● N–J (6)

	Calm	Force 1-4	Force 5-6	Force 7+	Sea temperatures (°F)	Remarks
SPRING						Malta shows how windy this Channel area can be and how only in summer is there enough seabreeze pull to take over the local winds at all markedly. Otherwise there are fresh to strong winds from all round the clock, especially during the days of spring. Statistics from the local sea area show the NW summer 'monsoon' and only during summer afternoons is this shifted to N and NE at Valetta by sea-breeze force.
Morn.	Few	W-NW all	All (14)	W-NW/E-SE (1)	M 58	
Aft.	Few	NE-N but all	All (20)	NW-SW (2)	A 60	
Eve.	Occ.	W-NW but all	All (13)	W-NW/NE (1)	M 65	
SUMMER						
Morn.	Occ.	NW-N but all	W-NW (4)	W (1)	J 70	
Aft.	Few	N-NE but all	W-N/SE (6)	W-NW (1)	J 75	
Eve.	Occ.	W-N but all	W-NW/E-S (7)	W-NW (1)	A 78	
AUTUMN						
Morn.	Occ.	W-NW but all	All (s-se) (5)	NW (1)	S 76	
Aft.	Few	N-E but all	All (4)	SW-NW (1)	O 73	
Eve.	Occ.	W but all	All (se) (7)	SW-S/NE (1)	N 67	

WINDS AND SEA TEMPERATURES AT BIZERTE

○ Jy–A (22) ● N (8)

	Calm	Force 1-4	Force 5-6	Force 7+	Sea temperatures (°F)	Remarks
SPRING						The African shore of the Sicilian narrows is very windy with strong to gale force winds mainly from NW or SE (or directions close to these). However, the calm mornings are followed by the growth of a phenomenal seabreeze on many spring and summer days that makes 20+ knots quite regularly and can grow to gale force. These winds lose strength by evening but still continue to blow.
Morn.	Many	W-NW (n-ne/se)	NW-SW/E-SE (12)	W-SW (4)	M 58	
Aft.	Occ.	W-NW/NE (sw-s)	All (sw-s) (25)	W-SW (3)	A 60	
Eve.	Occ.	W-NE (sw-se)	W-NW/NE-SE (20)	NW-SW/NE-E (5)	M 63	
SUMMER						
Morn.	Many	W-NW (n-ne/s)	All (s) (8)	W-SW (1)	J 69	
Aft.	Few	W-NE only	W-NE (24)	W-NW (3)	J 74	
Eve.	Occ.	W-NE only	W-NW/NE-E (17)	W-NW/E-SE (2)	A 77	
AUTUMN						
Morn.	Many	All (n-e)	All (n-e) (7)	W (1)	S 75	
Aft.	Occ.	All	W-NW/E-SE (20)	NW-SW (4)	O 71	
Eve.	Many	All (s)	W-NW/E-SE (15)	W-NW/E-SE (3)	N 66	

The instep and heel of Italy (*see Map 14*)

GENERAL FEATURES

The toe of Italy is very high and unfrequented. Only around the Gulf of Taranto do the mountains pull back leaving the heel of Italy quite low by comparison. This low coast continues from the Strait of Otranto up the Adriatic to beyond M. Gargano. From then on the mountains come, once again, down to the sea.

MAJOR WINDS

The prevailing wind is the NW–N 'monsoon' out of the Adriatic and across the Calabrian mountains and the Apennines. This wind shows up regularly in late spring and summer and only in autumn do easterlies become evident. Sometimes the wind is the tail end of bora from the top of the Adriatic, and, of course, southerlies bring the dust and heat of the scirocco.

WINDS AND SEA TEMPERATURES AT TARANTO

○ Jy–A (21) ● N–F (10)	Calm	Force 1–4	Force 5–6	Force 7+	Sea temperatures (°F)	Remarks
SPRING						Fresh winds at Taranto tend to come from all directions with equal regularity except in summer when E-NE is not favoured. The seabreeze is evident in spring and dominant in summer but few last into the evening. There are still many breezes in the afternoon in autumn which take over from a strong trend to gentle easterlies in the mornings.
Morn.	Many	W but all	All (w) (9)	NE (1)	M 57	
Aft.	Few	S-SW (n-e)	All (16)	N (3)	A 60	
Eve.	Occ.	All	All (e) (10)	SW-SE (2)	M 64	
SUMMER						
Morn.	Many	W-SW (n-ne/se)	All (ne-e) (5)	N (1)	J 69	
Aft.	Few	S-SW (e-se)	SW-SE/NW-N (12)	N (1)	J 76	
Eve.	Occ.	All	All (w) (8)	NW (1)	A 77	
AUTUMN						
Morn.	Many	E (sw)	All (5)	N/S-SE (1)	S 75	
Aft.	Occ.	S-SW	SW-SE/NW-NE (10)	All (w-nw) (2)	O 71	
Eve.	Occ.	E but all	All (9)	N/SW (2)	N 65	

WINDS AND SEA TEMPERATURES AT BRINDISI

○ Jy–A (24) ● N–F (10)	Calm	Force 1–4	Force 5–6	Force 7+	Sea temperatures (°F)	Remarks
SPRING						Brindisi on the Adriatic coast shows the strong mountain wind trend in the mornings (as well as other times of day). We have no statistics for the afternoon but can expect a NE-E seabreeze on many occasions that fails to keep the NW wind at bay into the evening. Compared to other places this part of Italy does not show a super-strong seabreeze regime. Bari shows much the same features where again the NW wind predominates and not many seabreezes can force their way in against it.
Morn.	Many	NW (ne-e)	NW-N/S-SE (10)	NW-NE/SW-S (2)	M 56	
Aft.	No data	No data	No data	No data		
Eve.	Many	All (w/e)	NW-N/SW-S (5)	W-SE/N (4)	M 64	
SUMMER						
Morn.	Many	NW (e-se/w)	NW-N (15)	NW-N/S (2)	J 69	
Aft.	No data	No data	No data	No data	J 75	
Eve.	Many	NW-N (w/e-se)	NW-N/SW (7)	NW-N/SW (2)	A 77	
AUTUMN						
Morn.	Many	N-SW (e-ne)	NW-NE (5)	S-E/NW (1)	S 73	
Aft.	No data	No data	No data	No data	O 69	
Eve.	Many	All (e-ne)	NW-N/S (5)	All (w-se) (3)	N 62	

Adriatic Coast of Italy: M. Gargano to Venice (see Maps 14–15)

GENERAL FEATURES

From M. Gargano that forms a sort of dew-claw on the heel of Italy up to Rimini the deeply fissured foothills of the Apennines come down to the sea. Then the great delta of the River Po opens up with many lagoons, terminating in the Laguna Veneta in which Venice stands.

MAJOR WINDS

The winds come down off the Apennines in the mornings and often stem the seabreezes leading to midday calms. There is the feed over the Apennines of the summer 'monsoon' as well as the inflow of the bora-type winds from the north or NE. All the near gale or stronger winds come from between NW and NE and the coast is somewhat sheltered from the scirocco.

WINDS AND SEA TEMPERATURES AT ANCONA

○ Jy-A (19) ● D-J (13)	Calm	Force 1-4	Force 5-6	Force 7+	Sea temperatures (°F)	Remarks
SPRING						Ancona is typical of the long Apennine coast of Adriatic Italy. There are many calms, even in the middle of the day, but this just reflects the war between the wind from the mountains and the wind from the sea which often reaches stalemate. This is not a coast if you want fresh winds but for water sports generally it has great appeal.
Morn.	Many	W (ne)	All (s-se) (6)	N-E (2)	M 54	
Aft.	Many	E (sw)	N-E/W (2)	—	A 58	
Eve.	Many	All	All (6)	NW-NE (2)	M 62	
SUMMER						
Morn.	Many	W (ne)	NW-SW/SE-E (2)	—	J 68	
Aft.	Occ.	N/E	NW-N/SE (2)	NW-N (1)	J 72	
Eve.	Many	S (sw)	NW-SW (2)	—	A 76	
AUTUMN						
Morn.	Many	W-S (n-ne)	All (e-se) (4)	NW-NE (1)	S 73	
Aft.	Often	All	NW-N/S (3)	—	O 67	
Eve.	Many	All	All (se) (5)	N-NE (2)	N 59	

WINDS AND SEA TEMPERATURES AT VENICE

○ Jy-A (12) ● N-M (12)	Calm	Force 1-4	Force 5-6	Force 7+	Sea temperatures (°F)	Remarks
SPRING						At Venice the morning N to NE winds come from the Dolomites but these are swept away by a SE-S seabreeze when they are not too strong – which is mostly. Apart from autumn mornings, when a southerly wind blows, the stronger winds are mainly from between NE and SE and are outpourings of bora from the Dinaric Alps opposite. The bora blows in a well defined corridor from the Trieste gap so that winds may fall from, say, Force 6-7 in the corridor to 3-4 outside it within a short distance.
Morn.	Often	NE-N (w)	NE-SE (5)	NE-E (1)	M 50	
Aft.	Occ.	SE-S (w-n)	NE-S (8)	NE-E (1)	A 57	
Eve.	No data	No data	No data	No data	M 62	
SUMMER						
Morn.	Occ.	N-E (w)	N-NE (3)	—	J 69	
Aft.	Few	SE-S (w-ne)	N-E-S (5)	NE (1)	J 73	
Eve.	No data	No data	No data	No data	A 78	
AUTUMN						
Morn.	Occ.	N-NE (s-se/w)	N-E/S-SW (6)	NE/S (1)	S 71	
Aft.	Occ.	All	NE-SE (6)	NE-SE (2)	O 64	
Eve.	No data	No data	No data	No data	N 58	

Adriatic Coasts of Yugoslavia (see Map 15)

GENERAL FEATURES

From Trieste southwards the mountains stand close to the coast. Between Pula and Dubrovnik there are many offshore islands and in some places a coastal plain.

MAJOR WINDS

The most dangerous wind of the area is the bora, a falling mountain wind from the Dolomites to the north and the (more important) Dinaric Alps along the coast. It blows strongest over the coast and drops in speed offshore. Opposing this trend there is a strong seabreeze force aided by anabatics up the mountain slopes.

NOTES

The curious effect of maximum wind speeds at around 10a.m. and in the late evening with a minimum in the afternoon is found elsewhere but nowhere more often than along this coast.

WINDS AND SEA TEMPERATURES AT TRIESTE

○ A (13) ● O-4p (10)

	Calm	Force 1-4	Force 5-6	Force 7+	Sea temperatures (°F)	Remarks
SPRING						The wind regime here is wind off the mountains whenever the seabreeze allows. There will be morning calms as the night wind off the mountains is stemmed and reversed by the seabreeze. Similarly in the late afternoon or early evening. However, the wind scene is dominated by often strong mountain wind i.e. bora.
Morn.	Some	NE-E (se-s)	NE-E (6)	NE-E (1)	M 50	
Aft.	Occ.	W-NW (s)	NE-E (4)	NE-E (1)	A 54	
Eve.	Often	E-SE (s/n)	NE-E (5)	NE-E (1)	M 62	
SUMMER						
Morn.	Occ.	SE/NW (n-s)	NE-E (2)	NE-E (1)	J 70	
Aft.	–	W-NW (s-se)	N-NE (1)	NE (1)	J 73	
Eve.	Many	SE-NE (n/s)	NE (1)	NE	A 76	
AUTUMN						
Morn.	Occ.	SE-NE (n/s)	NE-E (7)	NE (1)	S 70	
Aft.	Occ.	NW-SW/NE-SE	NE-E (4)	NE (1)	O 60	
Eve.	Many	SE-NE only	NE-E (7)	NE (1)	N 60	

WINDS AND SEA TEMPERATURES AT SPLIT

○ A (17) ● D (13)

	Calm	Force 1-4	Force 5-6	Force 7+	Sea temperatures (°F)	Remarks
SPRING						Split is pretty typical of the high Yugoslavian coast with a large proportion of strong winds from the Alps opposed by the seabreeze, so that on summer afternoons no less than two-thirds of the days have a light wind from SE. The off-shore wind and seabreeze directions will obviously differ somewhat at other places depending on the lie of the land.
Morn.	Many	NE (s-nw)	N-SE (15)	NE/SE (8)	M 57	
Aft.	Seldom	SE-S (nw-n)	NE-S (18)	NE-SE (7)	A 59	
Eve.	Many	All	N-SE (15)	NE/SE (8)	M 63	
SUMMER						
Morn.	Many	NE (sw-nw)	N-SE (9)	NE/SE (3)	J 69	
Aft.	Seldom	SE-S (nw-se)	All (nw/e) (9)	NE/SE (2)	J 73	
Eve.	Many	All	N-SE (9)	NE/SE (2)	A 74	
AUTUMN						
Morn.	Occ.	NE-E (s-nw)	N-E-S (18)	NE/SE-SW (8)	S 71	
Aft.	Occ.	SW-S (nw-n)	N-E-S (18)	NE/SE-SW (8)	O 67	
Eve.	Many	NE (s-nw)	N-SE (18)	NE/S-SE (7)	N 63	

West Coast of Greece: Ionian Islands
(see Map 14)

GENERAL FEATURES

This coast is very broken and mountains stoop down to the sea. The islands are high in most cases but the major inroad is the Gulf of Corinth.

MAJOR WINDS

The northerlies out of the Strait of Otranto blow at all seasons but much shelter is to be found around the islands. In the southern part of the Ionian Sea summer sees winds predominantly from between W and N. The coast also stands directly in the path of the scirocco.

WINDS AND SEA TEMPERATURES AT ZAKINTHOS

○ Jy-A (25) ● N-F (9)	Calm	Force 1-4	Force 5-6	Force 7+	Sea temperatures (°F)	Remarks
SPRING						Zakinthos lies 10 miles off the northwest tip of Peloponneus. It is directly in the path of the NW 'monsoon' flow across the Ionian Sea and so represents mainly exposed places on this coast of Greece. Its winds are predominantly NW at all seasons and in summer over half the winds that blow come from this direction and are light. What few gales there are are scirocco in spring or seabreeze enhanced NW 'monsoon'.
Morn.	Occ.	NW–SW (e)	NW–E/S (8)	N–NE/S (1)	M 59	
Aft.	Seldom	NW (e)	All (16)	NE/S (1)	A 60	
Eve.	Seldom	NW–W (e)	NW–N/SE–S (11)	S (1)	M 64	
SUMMER						
Morn.	Occ.	NW	NW (1)	—	J 69	
Aft.	Seldom	NW (e)	W–N/S (7)	NW (1)	J 75	
Eve.	Seldom	NW (e)	NW–N (5)	NW (1)	A 78	
AUTUMN						
Morn.	Occ.	W–NW (sw)	NW–NE/S–SE (10)	—	S 76	
Aft.	Seldom	NW–NE (e)	All (e–ne) (14)	—	O 78	
Eve.	Occ.	NW–SW (e/s)	All (e–ne) (9)	NE–E (1)	N 66	

WINDS AND SEA TEMPERATURES AT PATRAI

○ Jy-A (26) ● N-F (9)	Calm	Force 1-4	Force 5-6	Force 7+	Sea temperatures (°F)	Remarks
SPRING						Patrai on the north-facing coast of the Gulf of Corinth is representative of sheltered places close to mountains. To the south-east Panakhaikon rises to 6,000 ft (1,926m). To the northwest across the Gulf Gkiona rises to over 8,000 ft (2,510m). So strong winds come from the mountains while mornings and evenings are often calm with a seabreeze up the Gulf from the west by day.
Morn.	Many	All	N–NE (1)	—	M 58	
Aft.	Occ.	W–SW (e–se)	S–W/N–NE (9)	S (1)	M 62	
Eve.	Many	All	S–W/N–NE (5)	NE (1)	M 66	
SUMMER						
Morn.	Many	All (nw/e)	—	—	J 74	
Aft.	Occ.	W–SW (ne–se)	W–SW/N–NE (6)	W (1)	J 76	
Eve.	Many	S–SW	S (2)	—	A 78	
AUTUMN						
Morn.	Many	E (nw)	N (2)	—	S 74	
Aft.	Occ.	W–SW (e–se)	N/SE/SW (6)	SW (1)	O 71	
Eve.	Many	E–S (nw)	S–SW (2)	—	N 66	

Southwest Aegean: Sea of Crete
(see Map 16)

GENERAL FEATURES

The archipelago of the Kikladhes is tossed like a handful of a giant's playthings down from Athens towards Crete. Conditions on these islands will depend on exposure, on how large the island is and where they stand with respect to the prevailing Aegean winds. The mainland mountains often come close to the sea and coasts are rocky.

MAJOR WINDS

The capes of the southeast tips of Peloponnesus split the NW winds of the Ionian Sea from the NE winds down the southeast coasts of Greece. The island of Kithira has two predominant directions, W (as the Ionian wind comes round the capes) and NE as the wind down the Aegean spreads out on its way to North Africa. The latter are the 'etesians' and are the 'monsoon' of the Aegean that rises to its peak on the Turkish shore.

NOTES

The wind's season at Athens can be summed up as follows:

March }	Early seabreeze season
April }	
May }	Most seabreezes and fewest off-shore winds
June	No etesians
July	Early etesians
August	Etesians falter somewhat
September	Seabreezes falter
October	Etesians falter so seabreeze gains temporary mastery
November	Late seabreeze season

WINDS AND SEA TEMPERATURES AT MILOS

○ Jy-A (29) ● J (10)

	Calm	Force 1-4	Force 5-6	Force 7+	Sea temperatures (°F)	Remarks
SPRING						Milos shows the trends to expect on all the Kikladhes. Winds tend to blow one of two ways, either from N to NE or W to SW. Light winds predominate from northerly points throughout the season. The lack of light southerlies may be due to the fact that the anemometer was sheltered from this direction. However, there will not be many except when the scirocco blows.
Morn.	Some	N-NW (s)	N-NE/W-SW (1)	N-NE/ W-SW (3)	M 60	
Aft.	Occ.	NW (s)	N-NE/W-SW (12)	W-SW/N/ SE (4)	A 62	
Eve.	Some	All (s)	N-NE/W-SW (10)	N/SW (2)	M 66	
SUMMER						
Morn.	Some	N-NW (s-e)	All (s-e) (11)	N (1)	J 68	
Aft.	Occ.	NW-NE (s-e)	N-NE (12)	N-NE (1)	J 75	
Eve.	Some	N-NE (e-se)	N-NE/W-SW (8)	N (1)	A 74	
AUTUMN						
Morn.	Some	N (s)	N-NE/W-SW (13)	N-NE/W (3)	S 74	
Aft.	Occ.	All	All (e-se) (14)	N-NE/ W-SW (13)	O 72	
Eve.	Some	N (s)	N-NE/W-SW (10)	N-NE/ SW (1)	N 67	

WINDS AND SEA TEMPERATURES AT ATHENS

○ Jy-A (20) ● D-J (8)

	Calm	Force 1-4	Force 5-6	Force 7+	Sea temperatures (°F)	Remarks
SPRING						Athens is well sheltered and is much like other sheltered places on this coast. The early mornings are dominated by calm but the wind gets up during the mornings and can be a spanking breeze by afternoon. By evening the calms settle again. The prevailing wind is down the Aegean from NE but strong seabreeze effects sometimes increase S to SE winds to fresh or more.
Morn.	Mainly	All (w/e)	NE/W (1)	—	M 57	
Aft.	Occ.	S-SW	All (4)	W/E (3)	A 62	
Eve.	Many	All (e)	NE/SW (1)	—	M 65	
SUMMER						
Morn.	Mainly	N-NE (e-se)	N-NE (1)	—	J 71	
Aft.	Few	SW-S (e-se)	NW-NE (3)	NE (1)	J 77	
Eve.	Many	NE/SW (e)	NE (1)	—	A 76	
AUTUMN						
Morn.	Many	NE (w-nw)	N-NE (2)	NE (1)	S 74	
Aft.	Occ.	SW-S/NE (e)	N-NE/SW-S (4)	NE (1)	O 69	
Eve.	Many	NE (w-nw)	N-NE/SW (2)	NE (1)	N 62	

Northern Aegean (see Map 17)

GENERAL FEATURES

Mountains surround the Northern Aegean on all sides and the only large-scale opening is where the Dardenelles look through into the Sea of Marmara. On the whole the islands are larger and more scattered than further south. There are numerous openings into the mountains where rivers run to the sea but the coasts are mainly rocky.

MAJOR WINDS

The predominant wind directions are around north at all seasons rising to a peak of frequency in autumn after-noons. However, the region is a very windy one – not as windy as further south but still much windier than on Atlantic coasts.

WINDS AND SEA TEMPERATURES AT SKIROS

○ Jy-A (29) ● D-J (8)	Calm	Force 1-4	Force 5-6	Force 7+	Sea temperatures (°F)	Remarks
SPRING						Skiros is typical of the islands on the Greek side of the Northern Aegean. It has few calms and your chances of having quite a lot of Force 5 or more winds is high at any time of year.
Mom.	Few	All	N-NE/S but all (18)	N-NE/S (2)	M 57	
Aft.	Few	All (sw)	NW-NE/S but all (21)	N-NE/ S-SW (2)	A 59	
Eve.	Occ.	All	N-NE/S but all (16)	N-NE/ SW-S (2)	M 63	
SUMMER						
Mom.	Occ.	N-NE (s-sw)	W-NE (sw-e) (20)	N-NE (1)	J 69	
Aft.	Few	NW-SE (s-w)	NE-N but all (23)	N/S (1)	J 72	
Eve.	Occ.	NW (ne)	S-N (ne-se) (13)	N-NE (1)	A 74	
AUTUMN						
Mom.	Occ.	All	N-NE but all (24)	N-NE (1)	S 71	
Aft.	Few	All (w-sw)	N-NE but all (25)	N (1)	O 67	
Eve.	Occ.	All	N-NE but all (19)	NE-E/S (1)	N 62	

WINDS AND SEA TEMPERATURES AT ALEXANDROUPOLIS

○ Jy-A (18) ● D/Mr (11)	Calm	Force 1-4	Force 5-6	Force 7+	Sea temperatures (°F)	Remarks
SPRING						Alexandroupolis is close to the Turkish border. The mountains of Thrace die out here and leave a gap for the entry of winds from the Stranca mountains border-ing the Black Sea. The gap lies to the northeast so strong winds tend to come from there. However, spring and summer see half the daytime winds from the sea, but these have largely died by evening.
Mom.	Often	N-NE	All (w-nw) (9)	NE (1)	M 54	
Aft.	Few	SW (nw)	All (sw) (13)	N-NE (1)	A 57	
Eve.	Occ.	All (se)	All (w-nw) (9)	NE/S (1)	M 62	
SUMMER						
Mom.	Occ.	NE-SE (w-nw)	N-NE (8)	N/S (1)	J 68	
Aft.	Few	SW (nw/e)	All (s) (14)	NW-N (1)	J 74	
Eve.	Many	SW-W/NE (e-s)	N-NW/S (4)	—	A 74	
AUTUMN						
Mom.	Occ.	N-NW (s-sw)	N-NE (s-sw) (9)	N/S (1)	S 70	
Aft.	Occ.	NE/SW (w-nw)	All (nw) (14)	N/S-SW (2)	O 66	
Eve.	Many	N-NE (se)	N-NE/S-SW (8)	N-NE/S (2)	N 61	

Turkish Coast of the Aegean (*see Map 16*)

GENERAL FEATURES

A whole chain of often large Greek islands stretches down this mountainous coastline and these tend to lie as extensions broken away from high promontories. Thus the coast and its islands will have a wide variety of different conditions whose effects can only be gauged on the spot.

MAJOR WINDS

On the Grecian shore there is often war between the etesians and the seabreeze whereas on this shore there is often cooperation. The prevailing wind throughout the year is therefore NW, being seabreeze onto the lower-lying parts of the coastline aided by the etesians when they begin to blow in summer. Also allow for funnelling through between islands or the mainland.

WINDS AND SEA TEMPERATURES AT SAMOS

○ Jy-A (30) ● D-J (11)	Calm	Force 1-4	Force 5-6	Force 7+	Sea temperatures (°F)	Remarks
SPRING						Samos is typical of the islands on this side of the Aegean in that in spring light or calm mornings build to NW seabreeze by afternoon and die to light or calm by evening. However, with the help of the etesians in summer no other direction than NW is worth considering and moderate to strong afternoon winds appear every day lasting into the evening.
Mom.	Many	NW/All	NW-N/SE (7)	SE (1)	M 60	
Aft.	Occ.	NW (n-e)	W-NW/S-SE (10)	SE (1)	A 61	
Eve.	Many	All (e)	NW-N/SW-SE (10)	N/E (1)	M 64	
SUMMER						
Mom.	Many	NW only	NW-N (5)	—	J 69	
Aft.	Occ.	NW only	W-N (24)	—	J 71	
Eve.	Occ.	NW (w-sw/ne-e)	NW-N (6)	—	A 74	
AUTUMN						
Mom.	Many	NW/SE (w-sw)	NW-N/SE (3)	—	S 72	
Aft.	Occ.	NW (n-e)	NW/All (e-ne) (14)	NW (1)'	O 70	
Eve.	Many	NW-N (w-sw)	NW-N/SW-SE (6)	—	N 67	

WINDS AND SEA TEMPERATURES AT RHODES

○ Jy-A (30) ● D-J (9)	Calm	Force 1-4	Force 5-6	Force 7+	Sea temperatures (°F)	Remarks
SPRING						If sailboarders want Force 5 or more then Rhodes is the place to go in summer. There will be nothing but winds from W from Force 7 downwards right into the late evening. If you do not want those speeds leave this corner of Turkey alone. Some of this fixed speed and direction is due to funnelling between the high island and the high mainland which is worth noting for other islands also.
Mom.	Many	S (e-ne)	W-N/S-SE (12)	NW/S (1)	M 61	
Aft.	Occ.	W-NW (s-ne)	W-NW/S-E (21)	W-NW/SE (5)	A 62	
Eve.	Many	W (nw-e)	NW-SE (n-e) (14)	NW-SE (n-e) (3)	M 66	
SUMMER						
Mom.	Occ.	W only	W-N/S (7)	W-NW (1)	J 70	
Aft.	Few	W only	W only (37)	W (4)	J 79	
Eve.	Occ.	W only	W-N (13)	W/S (2)	A 80	
AUTUMN						
Mom.	Many	W (n-e/sw)	W-N/S-SE (5)	S (1)	S 78	
Aft.	Occ.	W (se-ne/sw)	W-NW/S-E (16)	W (1)	O 74	
Eve.	Many	W only	All (e-ne) (5)	W-NW (1)	N 68	

North African Coast: Egypt and Libya

(*see Map 18*)

GENERAL FEATURES

This is in general a low desert coast with higher ground coming close to the coast near Darnah (Jabal al Akhdar) and near Tripoli. Otherwise there is little to impede the wind.

MAJOR WINDS

This is the coast onto which the NW 'monsoon', which originates in the seas and mountains on the north side of the Mediterranean, blows. It is in general the coast of the great sea wind by day but also the coast of the scirocco.

WINDS AND SEA TEMPERATURES AT SALUM

	Calm	Force 1–4	Force 5–6	Force 7+	Sea temperatures (°F)	Remarks
○ *Jy–A (28)* ● *J (3)*						Representative of the desert shore, Salum, on the Gulf of Solum, lies close to the Egypt/ Libya border. The growth of the strong sea wind is evident in both spring and summer with half the winds that blow being from the sea and Force 5 or over in the afternoons of summer. Many of these winds are still blowing as late as 2000. Autumn shows the usual trend to have wind from many directions but the on-shore sea wind is still there.
SPRING						
Mom.	Occ.	All	All (e) (13)	S–W–N (4)	M 62	
Aft.	Occ.	N–E only	All (27)	S–W–N (5)	A 65	
Eve.	Occ.	N–E (s–w)	All (13)	SW/NW–N (2)	M 70	
SUMMER						
Mom.	Occ.	NW–N (sw–e)	NW–NE/SW–S (16)	W–N (1)	J 74	
Aft.	Few	N–E only	NW–NE (45)	NW–NE (4)	J 77	
Eve.	Few	N–NW (w–se)	NW–NE (19)	NW–N (1)	A 79	
AUTUMN						
Mom.	Occ.	NW (s–ne)	All (e–se) (9)	W–S (1)	S 79	
Aft.	Few	NE–N (s)	All (s–e) (24)	All (se–e) (3)	O 76	
Eve.	Occ.	N–NE	All (s–e) (7)	NW (1)	N 71	

WINDS AND SEA TEMPERATURES AT SIRTE

	Calm	Force 1–4	Force 5–6	Force 7+	Sea temperatures (°F)	Remarks
○ *Jy (23)* ● *N (4)*						Sirte, in the centre of the big bay that is the Gulf of Sidra, is a much quieter place than Salum further east. There is still an overwhelming number of days with sea-breeze but it is mostly light or gentle. This is because Sirte lies to the west of the corridor of strong NW winds that sweep into Libya and Egypt. For the western extensions of the North African coast see page 133.
SPRING						
Mom.	Occ.	W–S–E	S–SE/N–NW (10)	—	M 60	
Aft.	Few	NE–NW (se)	SW–E/NW–N (4)	—	A 61	
Eve.	Few	N–E (s)	N–E (3)	—	M 65	
SUMMER						
Mom.	Occ.	N/S	N (1)	—	J 70	
Aft.	Few	NW–NE only	NW–E (2)	—	J 77	
Eve.	Few	N–E only	N/E (2)	—	A 78	
AUTUMN						
Mom.	Occ.	SW–SE	N/S (1)	—	S 78	
Aft.	Few	NW–NE	N–W–S (3)	—	O 73	
Eve.	Occ.	N–E (w–sw)	NW–NE (2)	—	N 70	

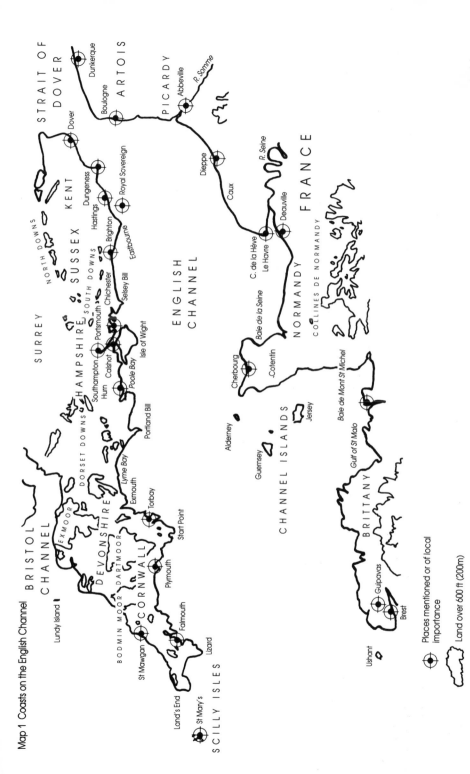

Map 1 Coasts on the English Channel

Map 2 The Solent

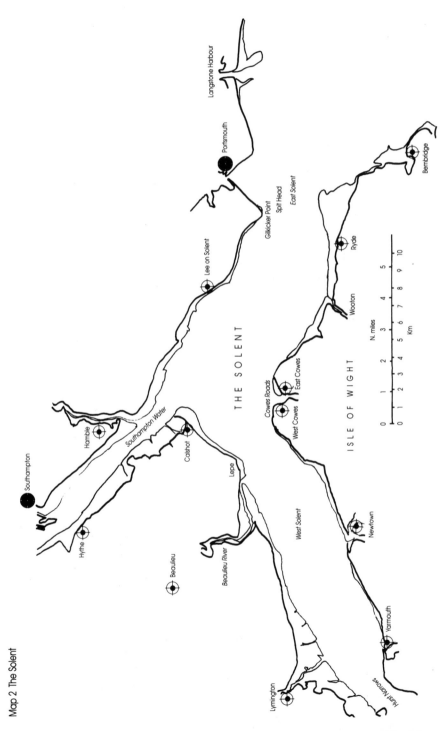

Map 3 North Sea Coast of England

NORTH SEA

Tynemouth

Newcastle

R. Tees

Scarborough

VALE OF PICKERING

YORKSHIRE WOLDS

YORKSHIRE

Hull

Spurn Point

LINCOLNSHIRE

The Wash

N O R F O L K

Norwich

Gorleston (Yarmouth)

King's Lynn

0   10   20   30   40   50   60   N. miles

0   20   40   60   80   100   Km

Places mentioned or of local importance

Cambridge

S U F F O L K

Ipswich

Colchester

CHILTERN HILLS

E S S E X

Southend

London

Shoeburyness

Thames Estuary

NORTH DOWNS

K E N T

Dover

154

Map 4 The Coasts of Scotland

Map 5 The West Coasts of England and Wales

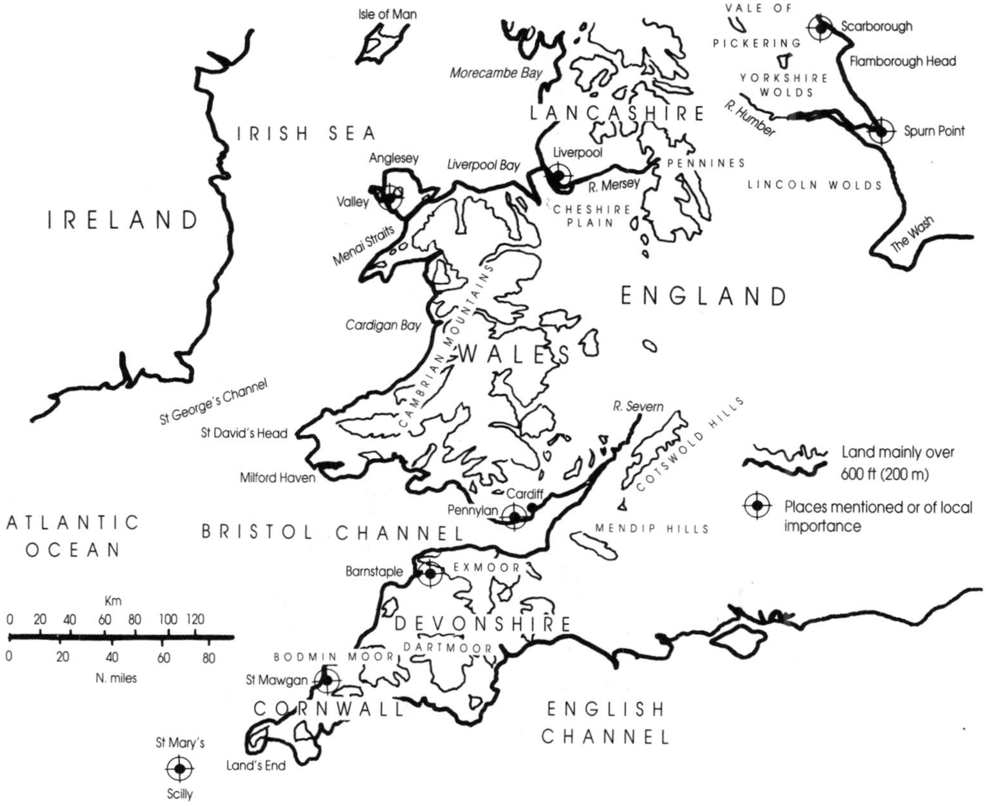

IRELAND

IRISH SEA

Isle of Man

St George's Channel

St David's Head

Milford Haven

ATLANTIC OCEAN

BRISTOL CHANNEL

Morecambe Bay

LANCASHIRE

Liverpool

R. Mersey

CHESHIRE PLAIN

Liverpool Bay

Anglesey

Valley

Menai Straits

Cardigan Bay

CAMBRIAN MOUNTAINS

WALES

Cardiff

Penryn

ENGLAND

PENNINES

VALE OF PICKERING

YORKSHIRE WOLDS

R. Humber

LINCOLN WOLDS

Scarborough

Flamborough Head

Spurn Point

The Wash

R. Severn

COTSWOLD HILLS

MENDIP HILLS

EXMOOR

DEVONSHIRE

DARTMOOR

BODMIN MOOR

CORNWALL

Barnstaple

St Mawgan

Land's End

ENGLISH CHANNEL

St Mary's

Scilly

Land mainly over 600 ft (200 m)

Places mentioned or of local importance

Km
0   20   40   60   80   100 120

N. miles
0   20   40   60   80

155

156

Map 6 The Coasts of Ireland

0   10   20   30   40   50   60   N. miles
0   20   40   60   80 100   Km

⊕ Places mentioned or of local importance

Land mainly over 600 ft (200 m)

ATLANTIC OCEAN

NORTH CHANNEL

Jura

Islay

Kintyre

Arran

Malin Head

Isle of Man

IRISH SEA

WALES

NORTHERN IRELAND

ANTRIM MOUNTAINS

Belfast

Strangford Lough

Lough Foyle

Donegal Bay

Belmullet

Clew Bay

Galway Bay

R. Shannon

SOUTHERN IRELAND

Dublin

WICKLOW MOUNTAINS

Wexford

Killarney

BOGGERAH MOUNTAINS

Cork

Cork Harbour

Roche Point

Fastnet Rock

Map 7 The North Sea Coasts of Holland and West Germany

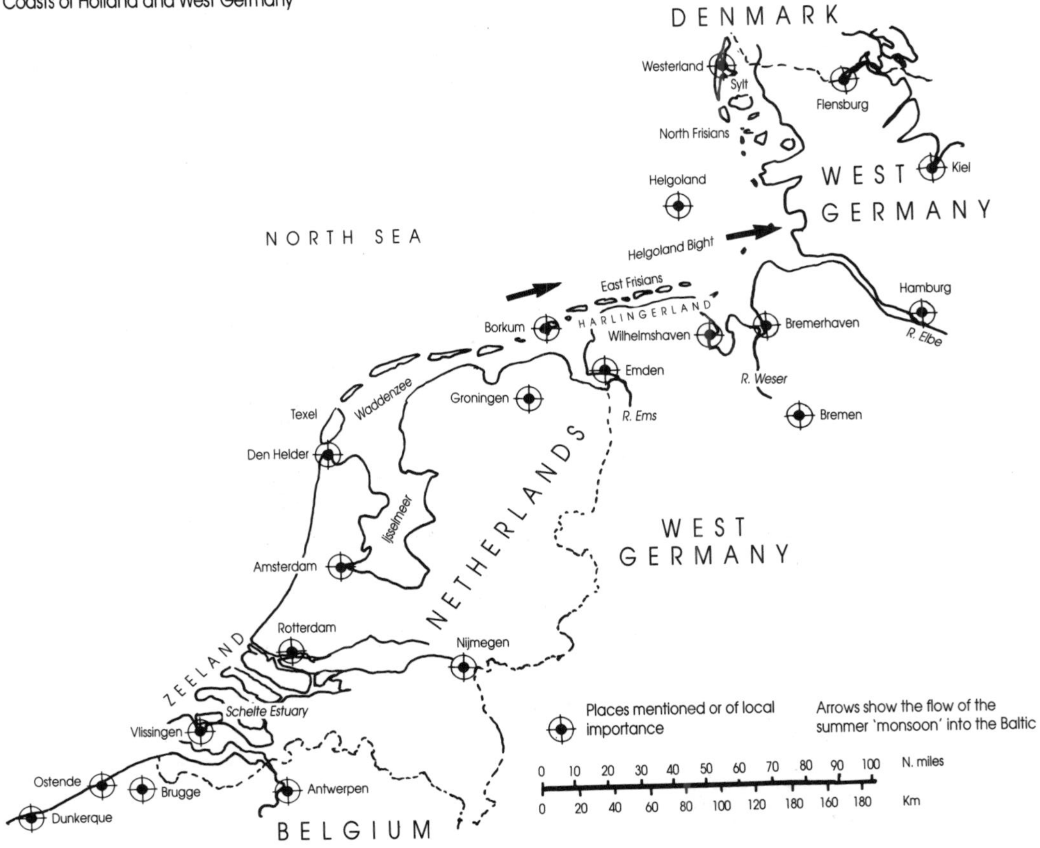

DENMARK

WEST GERMANY

Flensburg
Kiel

Westerland
Sylt
North Frisians

Helgoland
Helgoland Bight

Hamburg
R. Elbe

Bremerhaven
R. Weser

Bremen

East Frisians

H A R L I N G E R L A N D

Wilhelmshaven

Emden
R. Ems

Borkum

Groningen

NORTH SEA

Waddenzee

IJsselmeer

NETHERLANDS

WEST GERMANY

Nijmegen

Texel

Den Helder

Amsterdam

Rotterdam

Antwerpen

Schelde Estuary

Z E E L A N D

Vlissingen

Brugge

Ostende

Dunkerque

BELGIUM

Places mentioned or of local importance

Arrows show the flow of the summer 'monsoon' into the Baltic

N. miles
0   10   20   30   40   50   60   70   80   90   100

Km
0   20   40   60   80   100   120   140   160   180

MAPS

157

Map 8 The Baltic Coasts of Scandinavia

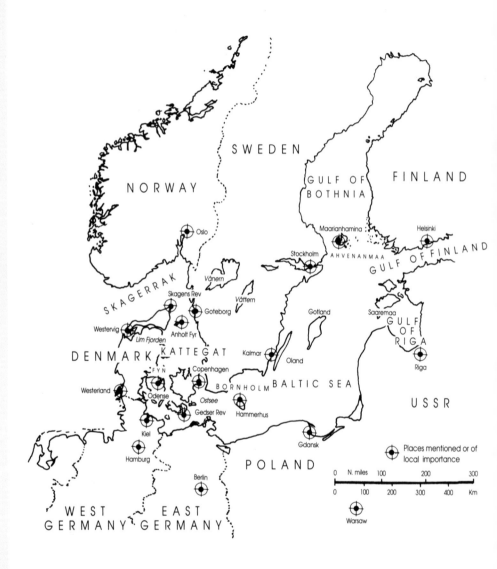

Map 9 The Bay of Biscay

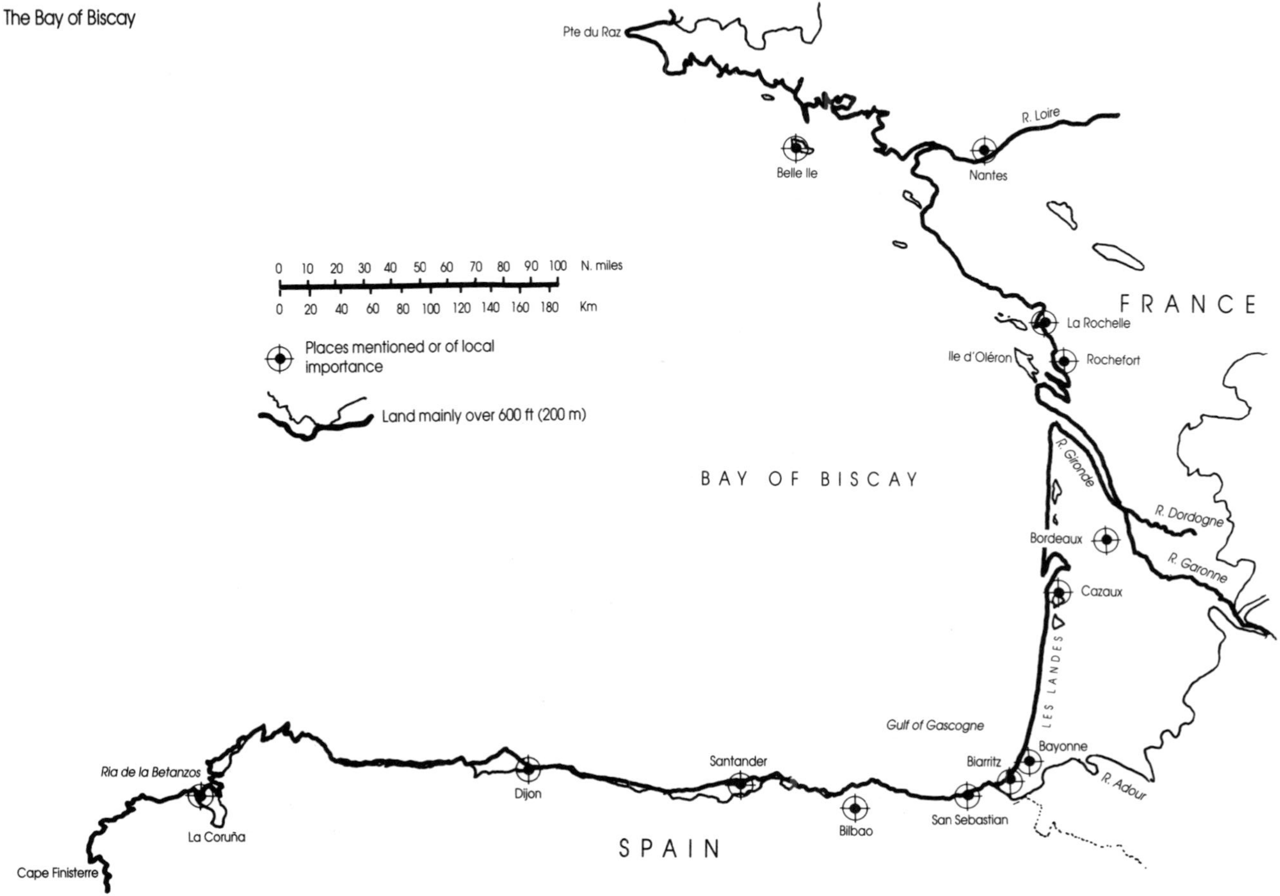

FRANCE

R. Loire

Nantes

La Rochelle

Rochefort

Ile d'Oléron

Belle Ile

R. Gironde

Bordeaux

R. Dordogne

R. Garonne

Cazaux

LES LANDES

R. Adour

Bayonne

Biarritz

San Sebastian

Bilbao

Gulf of Gascogne

BAY OF BISCAY

Santander

SPAIN

Dijon

Pte du Raz

Rio de la Betanzos

La Coruña

Cape Finisterre

N. miles
Km

Places mentioned or of local importance

Land mainly over 600 ft (200 m)

0   10   20   30   40   50   60   70   80   90   100

0   20   40   60   80   100   120   140   160   180

Map 10 The Atlantic Coasts of Spain and Portugal

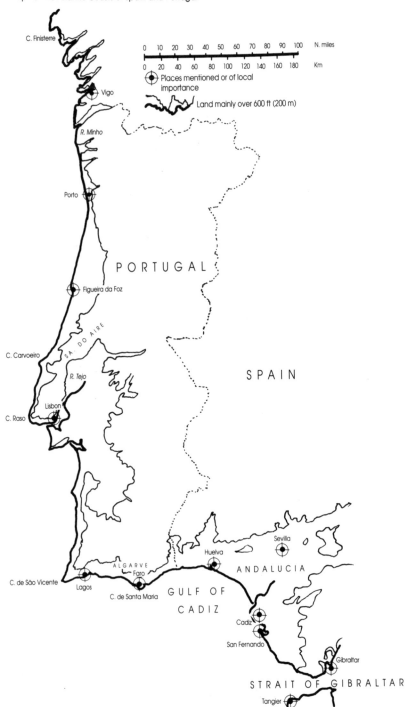

Map 11 The Mediterranean Coasts of Spain and the Balearics

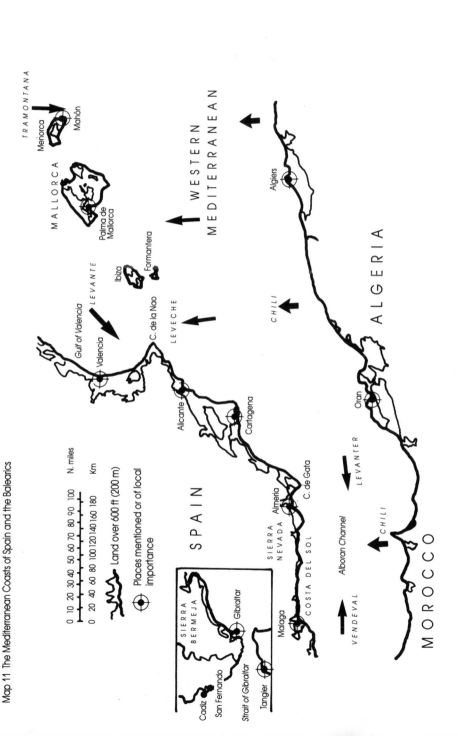

Map 12 The Mediterranean Coasts of France and Italy

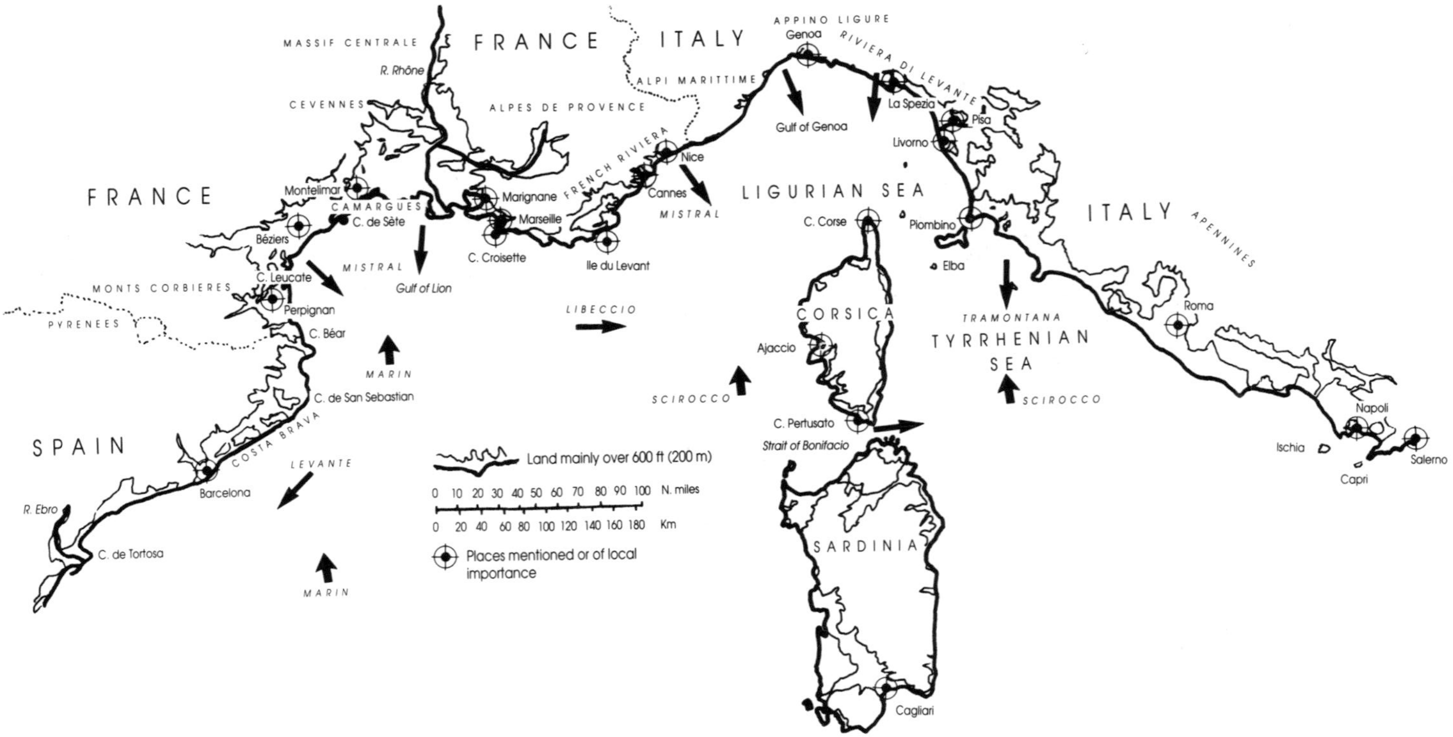

M A S S I F   C E N T R A L E

C E V E N N E S

MONTS CORBIERES

P Y R E N E E S

FRANCE

F R A N C E   ITALY

ALPI MARITTIME

ALPES DE PROVENCE

APPINO LIGURE

ITALY

APENNINES

RIVIERA DI LEVANTE

R. Rhône

Montélimar

Béziers

C. Leucate

Perpignan

C. Béar

C. de San Sebastian

C A M A R G U E S

C. de Séte

Marignane

Marseille

C. Croisette

Ile du Levant

Cannes

Nice

Genoa

Gulf of Genoa

La Spezia

Livorno

Pisa

Plombino

Elba

Roma

Napoli

Salerno

Capri

Ischia

Cagliari

FRENCH RIVIERA

MISTRAL

MISTRAL

MISTRAL

LIBECCIO

MARIN

MARIN

MARIN

Gulf of Lion

Barcelona

C. de Tortosa

R. Ebro

COSTA BRAVA

COSTA LEVANTE

SPAIN

LIGURIAN SEA

SCIROCCO

SCIROCCO

CORSICA

C. Corse

Ajaccio

C. Pertusato

Strait of Bonifacio

SARDINIA

TYRRHENIAN SEA

TRAMONTANA

SCIROCCO

〰〰〰 Land mainly over 600 ft (200 m)

0 10 20 30 40 50 60 70 80 90 100 N. miles

0 20 40 60 80 100 120 140 160 180 Km

⊕ Places mentioned or of local importance

162

Map 13 The Coasts of Sicily and the toe of Italy

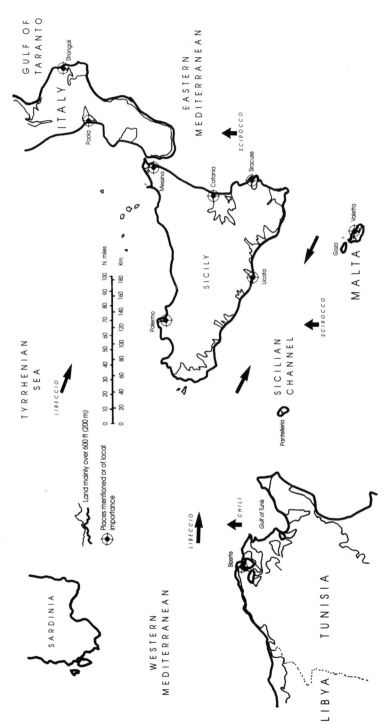

Map 14 The Coasts of the Ionian Sea

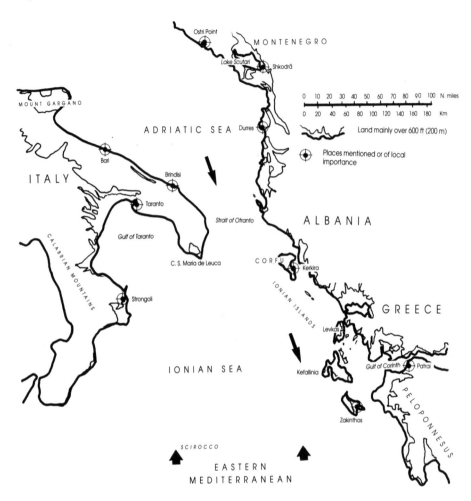

Map 15 The Coasts of the Adriatic

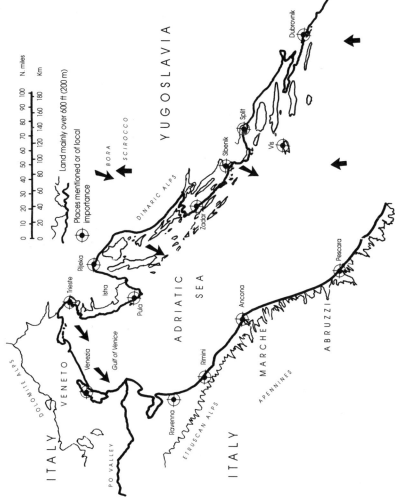

166

Map 16 The Islands of Greece and the South Aegean Sea

Map 17 The Coasts of the North Aegean Sea

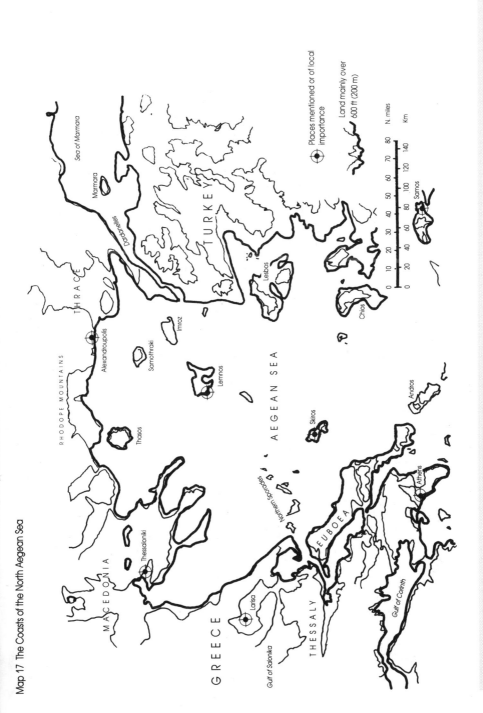

Places mentioned or of local importance

Land mainly over 600 ft (200 m)

N. miles

Km

Sea of Marmara

Marmara

Dardanelles

THRACE

RHODOPE MOUNTAINS

Alexandroupolis

Samothraki

Imroz

TURKEY

Lemnos

Thasos

Lesbos

AEGEAN SEA

Chios

Samos

MACEDONIA

Thessaloniki

Skiros

Andros

Northern Sporades

EUBOEA

GREECE

Larisa

THESSALY

Gulf of Salonika

Gulf of Corinth

Athens

Map 18 The North African Coast

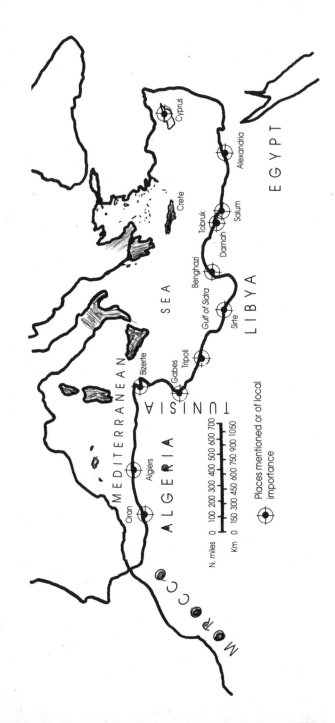

EGYPT

Alexandria

Salum
Tobruk
Damah
Cyprus

Crete

Benghazi
Gulf of Sidra

LIBYA

Sirte

MEDITERRANEAN

SEA

Tripoli
Gabes
Bizerte

TUNISIA

ALGERIA

Algiers

Oran

MOROCCO

N. miles 0 100 200 300 400 500 600 700
Km 0 150 300 450 600 750 900 1050

Places mentioned or of local
importance